S.H

Se

Healing

Energy

By

Oro Selket

C000070552

© **2006 Oro Selket – Farid Khattab.**
Email: oroselket@oroselket.com
Web site http://www.oroselket.com

No part of this book may be reproduced by any means
without the permission of the author.

ISBN: 1-4196-3445-3

Published by BookSurge Publishing

Thank You

Thank you God for allowing me to help people.

I definitely thank Vince Kaye for all his teachings and continuous guidance and help.

I also would like to thank all those who trusted me with their pains and discomfort and allowed me to help them with Energy Balance.

Table of Contents

Introduction

The information and methods presented here are sufficient to allow you to practice Energy Balance successfully, and have a good working self healing energy.

Several topics are covered, the first being what is self healing energy, that we all have, and how it affects us, and how people get sick, then pollution types that immensely, weaken the - S.H.E. - self healing energy, and then the methods to fix the energy imbalance, methods are; energy balance, advanced energy balance, energy balance for animals, birds, plants and places, color balance, relaxation methods, exorcism, hypnosis, line body parts balance, visualization, power of the mind, listenology, psychic surgery. Some diseases are selected to emphasize the pollution effects, and how to deal with them, for example, cancer, autism and syndromes, allergies, headaches and migraine headaches, arthritis, aging, and back pain.

Then several guidelines for understanding numbers and studies, and what is dead and live food, how to eat based on ROYGBIV, and what is success.

Very interesting topics that are also discussed are; remote viewing, when did things happen, protection from whatever affects the performance of the S.H.E., memory, how to communicate what is best for you to your master chip.

All this knowledge comes with a responsibility that when handled properly, will enhance your S.H.E., we discuss a day's anatomy and how our master chip is invaded.

More topics, like ball of energy and how to use it, and the human radar use in case of emergencies, and also how to utilize sleep so we can increase our wake up time value by up to 50%.

There are so many lab tests performed today to check the blood and urine and several other constituents, it will be shown how to achieve your best ideal numbers for you and for the benefit of the S.H.E., there are so many diseases mentioned and we provide Orothemes which are energy balanced images to help improve conditions, as well as covering the various human body parts and organs.

Preventative measures and daily power exercises are also covered for the benefit of the self healing energy.

Stress is covered at that later stage, hoping that when you have reached that part of the book, you would be stress free.

I have read so many books, and I have listed the most valuable to me, and the ones that helped in many ways, also mentioned some useful web sites for getting more information.

Every human, animal and plant has a self healing energy that is unique to itself; in fact every object that is alive has a S.H.E..

Self healing energy performs many functions during a course of a twenty four hour period, and we don't even know that this self healing energy is performing its functions, cells die and cells get weak and those are replaced and fixed automatically, in the human body there are over a trillion cells, all communicating and working together in harmony for the welfare of the being.

The self healing energy has limits to its functionality, and when those limits are reached it is slowed down, and symptoms start to occur.

Most people as soon as there is a symptom start thinking of the worst possible diseases and think of their need to see a doctor and get a prescription. This thinking process in itself is self defeating and makes the self healing energy performance stay at those limits that caused the symptoms to appear, we will cover the thinking pollution and how to avoid it and protect yourself, for the ultimate benefit of your self healing energy.

People visit a doctor, who prescribes a medication and tells them to rest, the rest in itself provides enough time for the self healing energy to be restored to its normal full power, because one is away from the negative interactions on the electromagnetic frequency level, helped by your positive thoughts that you are and will get better.

Let us analyze, what happened in the above example of getting a symptom, and place equal weighting on each of the three items. The medication 1/3 and resting 1/3 and the positive thought 1/3, you will notice that 2/3 could have been achieved easily by yourself, and there are doubts as to the remaining 1/3 if it did anything, because, with over a trillion cells in our bodies, there is no way of knowing how this medication performed overall, what is the effect on every cell in the body, even with all of today's technology, it would be cost prohibitive to even try to make such a test with all the possible combinations of cells interactions. There are of course guidelines, but they are not absolute. This is a personal opinion and legally I have to say follow your physician's advice, so follow your physician's advice.

Disclosure

The material provided here is for information purposes and doesn't replace the value of checking with your medical doctor when you need to. If you need to see your medical doctor always do that.

Chapter 1

Self Healing Energy, S.H.E.

Everything is made out of cells, and there is a master cell that regulates all cells' communications and interactions.

An example in the human species of the master cell work is our heart, lungs, intestine, liver and kidney, all function in harmony and perfectly during our sleep.

The master cell could be termed also master chip that is built in, it tolerates our mistakes, we get cut by a sharp object, it immediately sends signals to ease the pain, clot blood and repair the tissue, all this is done automatically, of course when the master chips limit is reached it still acts automatically but not as fast, and in some cases its actions are slowed due to other conditions, one of which is the mental state of the person.

Another example is when we bump against a chair or a piece of furniture or against anything we didn't see that was in our way.

The thought process that goes through one's mind is very important, as this is how the chip partly gets its messages, for example in certain situations when we trip an instantaneous thought comes to mind I am falling, so we do fall, as we have confirmed to the chip that we expect to fall, so why would the chip make a liar out of us, if instead we think I am not falling, or I am OK, we will not fall, the chip takes over the message and manipulates our muscles and actions to stop us from falling.

Read the above example again and compare it to what you do, all it takes is pure simple awareness of the presence of the master chip and what messages we feed it, once you are aware of this process, you can always say the right words and think the right thoughts, it might take several times to reach that desired effect, as don't forget you have been automatically feeding the chip the undesired messages for many years, because for sure on tripping you don't want to fall, but you fall because of the message you send to the chip.

The self healing energy works all the time, your input affects its performance, it is your message that affects the outcome, unfortunately we have been trained to react and give messages that produce the undesired effect.

So many of today's gestures and motions and thoughts and reactions have stemmed from the silent movie times, because at the time there was no sound in movies, however the director wanted to create an inference so viewers would understand what is going on, so many gestures were created by the creative directors, and unfortunately this continued after sound was included with movies, and people started imitating those gestures and mannerisms.

For example when a person is angry, they don't have to be vicious and frowning, but that was what was portrayed. When someone has an evil thought they showed them with actions and face portraying an ugly creature, it is normal to get evil thoughts, everyone gets them, but the difference is how we deal with them. Normal people brush them off and return to the right frame of mind, however a very small percentage of people hang on to that evil thought and sometimes are quite creative in doing that. That is how there are criminals, back stabbers. Some people talk about others and reveal secrets they have been entrusted with, all this is wrong, the proper way is to ask yourself can I say what I am saying in front of the person, if the answer is no, then you shouldn't say it, as a rule when you talk about someone either you say something good or don't say anything at all, a lot of problems are created from doing the wrong thing, and with all these wrong actions a lot of negative waves and frequencies are created, that definitely affect the master cell and our S.H.E., as when someone talks bad about us a negative frequency is created and it affects us.

In addition to the messages we send to the master chip, we also interfere with the process making it take longer, one time I had a runny nose, which is a healing process in itself to get rid of whatever the body doesn't want, many years ago I would have went to a drug store and spend an hour looking at the many suggested remedies to stop the fluid from coming out of my nose, and it would have taken days to clear the condition.

Now that I know better I decided to let it flow and let the body get rid of what it doesn't want, and within twenty four hours the fluid stopped coming out of my nose.

The point is the body had to get rid of something, and whether we like it or not it will get rid of it, the difference is in our action, I decided to let it finish the healing process, had I taken a medication it would have taken longer, because the medication stops the process of letting the fluid out until its effect goes away, then the healing starts again and so on, with a net result of suffering for a longer time.

We must be aware that there is a self healing energy that works for our benefit, and our thoughts and actions affect the duration and outcome.

I firmly believe that there is the most advanced pharmaceutical industry within our system which serves the self healing energy which is run by the master cell or chip.

A simple exercise that would do away with many ill feelings is a smile, even if you force yourself to smile, if you cannot do that just make your lips as if you are smiling, hang on to that lip position for a few minutes and then you will really smile from your heart, because you will either laugh at yourself for taking that lip position or you will actually feel the calmness and serenity that the smile gave you. With the smile many needed chemicals are produced within our body system, and many functions are completed successfully, like digestion, tissue repair in case we were cut, cell communication is normal with the ultimate result of many benefits. Very useful methods in case of headaches, instead of automatically reaching for a pill, do that simple exercise, and you will be happily surprised at what your S.H.E can do, and that is just the tip of the iceberg.

Next we discuss pollution and how it affects us in an adverse way, and how to deal with various types of pollutions.

Chapter 2

Pollution

Pollution has many synonyms, for example; contamination, corruption, fouling, misuse, and these are what we get when we are polluted. The effect is a lot greater than what can be sensed by our five senses, I firmly believe sickness is a result of pollution; pain is a result of pollution; sadness is a result of pollution; and stress is a major result of pollution, stress is usually self induced, instead of saying this is a stressful situation, better to say it is just a different situation that I am not familiar with or it is a set of conditions that are new to me, there is a purpose and a reason for this situation, simply at the onset we don't know the reason or purpose.

Every one has an upper and a lower limit, anything falling within those limits are handled successfully, however once those limits are crossed, either above the upper limit or below the lower limit, we become unbalanced and stress is self induced.

The logical procedure to adopt, is to figure out a way, devise a system, and think creatively to place everything that falls outside the limits within the upper and lower limits or guidelines, here all we have to do is either raise our upper limit and or lower the lower limit so the problem or situation is within the normal limits, or slice the problem so it is smaller pieces rather than a big one, so the pieces fit within our normal limits, or you can do a combination of both. When you adopt this logic to all situations, you will find that you no longer have problems, and no self induced stress, and your handling of situations is a lot more effective with very beneficial results for your well being.

When refusing to adopt that logic it is your choice and that is how self induced stress comes to the picture; that is why I say stress is most definitely self inflicted, like someone on purpose crossing the street without looking for incoming cars.

When we are presented with a situation, usually it is within our capability to resolve. Look back to your life, and see how many issues were resolved, look at a child and learn, they learn how to walk, despite the fact that they fall many times before they finally master walking. Children succeed because their minds are not polluted yet, for a child to walk, talk, climb and jump over things is really quite an accomplishment. Then they learn how to walk faster and then run and control themselves to stop when they need to.

Abolish from your dictionary words like problem and difficult, I will tell you how I did away with those words.

I gave the word problem a new meaning, professional blamer, you will notice the word problem could have been derived from the two words professional and blamer, for short Pro Blamer, and for even shorter problem, and since I don't like to blame anyone and I am not a professional blamer, then I no longer use that word.

For the word difficult, the new meaning is different cult, you will also notice that the word difficult could have originated from the two words different and cult, probably I am not correct as far as the English language goes on origin of the words, however this is what I devised to help abolish those words from my dictionary, and since I have my own cult that I am happy with, I don't need a different cult, and the word difficult is gone for ever.

An interesting incident that will demonstrate the validity of the above statements happened to me many years ago. At that time I was very good with computers, and I knew visual basic, which is a programming language, I had over a visitor who wanted to ask me about visual basic, as I started explaining things he started saying it is difficult, and he repeated that several times, at the same time my son; who was four years old at the time; was present with us and heard him say the word difficult, within me I was very furious for that word to be mentioned in front of my son.

To me anyone saying something is difficult is really putting the blame on something else and they are not to blame, and I wanted to correct this as fast as I can, because I don't want my son to grow up used to saying difficult and blaming other issues, like what some would say it is difficult what do you expect me to do, after that sincere desire to protect my son from this type of pollution, it was clear to me that difficult and easy don't really exist and they are just a cover up.

I explained to the visitor, that difficult doesn't mean very much, because what you are saying is that it is that thing that is difficult, despite the fact that it is easy for me, so how come can something be two things at the same time for different people, and when we say easy, we are very proud that something is easy for us, however the truth of the matter is that we say difficult to things we don't know and we say easy for things we know, so actually it is better to say I don't know rather than saying it is difficult, and think about it for second, whenever we don't know something we say it is difficult and once we know it we say it is easy, so how can the same thing be two things, difficult and easy for the same person within a certain span of time. The common denominator is knowledge, and I was very pleased that I came up with this observation mainly for my son's benefit, and ever since whenever there is an opportunity I explain this concept, please adopt that way and explain it to many people as circumstances allow.

And from there on, anybody telling me something is difficult, I know they don't understand or they don't know, and I handle the situation from that point, and start explaining again in a different way.

If you are with friends or at work, and you catch yourself saying the D word, you will get a better response if you say I don't understand, then others will either explain the matter to you or point you in the right direction to get the knowledge.

Remember that when you are telling someone that something is difficult you are presenting them with a problem, but if you say you don't understand, they will be glad to help you.

The above observation and concept removed a type of thought pollution that unfortunately many people are affected by.

Come up with your own observations and conclusions regarding those unwanted words and you will live a healthier life, and your S.H.E. will be working perfectly. If you do come up with such observations and play of words, I would like to hear from you, see how to contact me at the end of the book.

The immediate thought that comes to mind when the word pollution is mentioned is smog and car pollution, nobody ever thinks about thought pollution, now you know better.

Smog and car pollution are an issue now and has been for quite many years because the natural balance of nature has been impaired, for example trees have been cut, and normal flow of air currents was and is obstructed by buildings, we originally had a balanced state with its S.H.E. working for our benefit, and once we started to tamper with the balance, things started to affect us and make us sick.

The greater S.H.E., which could be the Earth's S.H.E. or the Galaxy's S.H.E., you can go as high as you want or as high as your mind will allow you to, is affected by other S.H.E.'s, the galaxy is made up of planets and stars, the earth is made up of land and water and the skies, the land has trees and underground resources, the ocean has fish and plants and animals, the list could go on and on, but that is not the place for this hierarchy of objects, we just have to acknowledge this fact, it is not only us as humans that have a S.H.E., animals, plants, winds, and the sky also have it. In fact everything has its S.H.E. and when a certain S.H.E. is tampered with it creates an imbalance in the larger S.H.E.

A point to remember is that sometimes we feel down for no apparent reason, it is highly probable that some S.H.E. in your immediate surroundings is imbalanced, and in turn the body picked up those signals. Once you know how to use the pendulum as you read on, go around your surroundings with the pendulum to identify where the imbalance is and fix it, you will notice the pendulum rotating anticlockwise, where the imbalance is, and all you have to do is rotate the pendulum clockwise to fix that imbalance. The imbalance is a break in the electromagnetic field of that object, the object could be another person, an animal, a plant, it could also be a greater imbalance coming from a distance, your neighbors, or even another street all together, you use the pendulum to know where it is coming from, if it is outside your immediate surroundings, you place a shield around you as mentioned in the Protection chapter as you read on.

You will notice me saying as you read on, because really everything is interrelated in one way or another, ideally read the whole book and then notice how matters fit together.

There are many pollutants, what was mentioned above is one type, thought pollution, however there are so many types and many pollutants, anything affecting a S.H.E. in an adverse way is a pollutant, and there are so many of those right now everywhere, it is unfortunate but true.

To do away with pollution and protect ourselves we need to know that there is pollution, some we cause ourselves and some are outside our control, some we can detect with our five senses and other types we cannot acknowledge with our five senses, I say five senses, because they are the commonly known senses at the conscious level, the sense of taste, hearing, seeing, smelling and touch, we all have more than five senses, at a different level from the conscious state, some might say sub-conscious, the prefix sub means under or below, which doesn't really do justice to that high powered level, some might call it super-conscious or supra-conscious, where the prefixes super and supra mean upper and above, I think the prefix ultra which means beyond is a lot more appropriate making it ultra-conscious.

It doesn't matter what that other level is called, just acknowledge the presence of another level that is highly developed and there are no tests or equipment to quantify it.

Those ultra-senses detect silently all other pollution types, which I call invisible pollution, and the way we are notified by the ultra-senses is totally different from the five senses notifications, examples of such notifications are; getting sick, feeling irritable for no apparent reason, over sleeping, missing an appointment, remembering something suddenly, flashes of inspiration to solve a problem, dreams, saying something that doesn't make sense to the conscious mind and when this happens, don't dismiss it, say it again and reason out the message, taking the wrong turn while driving, feeling pain, feeling uneasy.

The unfortunate side is that many of those messages pass by without being acknowledged, because we have been trained to dismiss them, I always say, things happen, and things occur for a reason, something might come across today, but doesn't get used till for example ten years later, and then we remember and say, now I know why. Trust your ultra-conscious for it is communicating with you to help you.

As mentioned earlier there are so many types of pollutants; however there is only one result, which is affecting the function and normal operation of our S.H.E..

I will classify pollution as below:

Thoughts, internal and external, verbal and silent, pollution

Actions, induced pollution

External visible pollution

External invisible pollution

Food Additives

Natural Pollution

Man made specific Pollution

Others

Knowing the culprits will help us avoid them, and protect ourselves.

A very clear example that shows the effects of those pollutants, is that viruses and bacteria are airborne and around us at all times, like the flu virus, many times we are exposed to someone who has a flu virus or a cold, and we don't get sick and other times we do get sick, the difference of how we are affected, depends on one or a combination of the above types of pollution, if we are being polluted we will get sick because the function of the S.H.E. is impaired, if we are not polluted and well protected we will not get sick.

Thoughts

We think all the time, it is a process that we do all our living lives, and also maybe after our living lives. We think while we are awake, we think while we are asleep, we think when we want to, we think when we don't want to, we think even when there is nothing to think about, like day dreaming.

The type of thoughts has a profound effect on our Self Healing Energy. Thoughts can help it perform better, or slow its performance or even stop it all together.

An example of such thoughts in action is, when you come close to someone or being in the same room with someone who has a cold who just coughed or sneezed, the immediate thought that 99% of people get, is, I will get the cold too, and they end up getting the cold, because this is what they just said to themselves, they just passed the wrong message to their master chip or master cell, if instead they would have thought to themselves I am immune to this virus, or I am protected, chances are they will not be infected with this virus.

All it takes is a split second thought. Realizing that your thoughts affect your well being, and you being a normal logical person, the obvious right thought should be I am immune, I am protected, or something similar to that, it takes just wanting to be good and healthy to catch yourself with the wrong thought and correcting it immediately, once you start realizing what you are thinking and correcting it several times, the right thoughts will become the normal thoughts that immediately come to mind, instead of the wrong thoughts, and you become on your way to join the 1% that think the correct thoughts.

It is quite a simple exercise with very rewarding, and beneficial results to your health and to your pocket. If you are managing a group of people, or have your own company, inform your employees of this thought process mechanism and you will have fewer sick leaves in your department or company and will have higher productivity. Apply the same principle in your home and protect your family, and explain it to your parents and or grandparents, to help them be in better health.

Thoughts come from you and can come from external sources, like other people, or from television or from the radio; you have to be careful what you are listening to.

The simple way to cancel the undesired effect of those external thoughts, is to replace them with a good thought, let us say someone tells you "you look pale", you should immediately correct that and say to yourself "I look great and feel good", it couldn't be any simpler than that to ward off the undesired effects, you definitely agree with me that it is quite simple.

Now you know what effects thoughts have on you, and you know how to correct any wrong thoughts, whether from you or from an external source. All it takes is your desire to be better.

Now one type of pollution is under your control and your S.H.E. will work better for you.

Actions

Actions are activities we do; we could do activities by choice and do other activities as a habit, or on impulse.

Actions by choice, like watching a TV show that is filled with wrong thoughts and the point here is that you know it is wrong thoughts, but you still watch it and listen to it, listening to idle chat on the radio or from friends, and many more activities you already do and are aware of, I am sure you know what is right and what is wrong.

Some people even talk to each other about those types of shows and even argue about them, thus increasing the effect of the pollution.

Other examples to actions by choice, using certain bad insulting words, calling people names, specially close ones, some call their children names, like fat, dumb, no good, even if you say it in a humorous way it still is a pollution and creates a negative surrounding for you and the children, others do the same with coworkers in the work place, also creating pollution at the work place, and the S.H.E. of the other person and the place and you are affected.

If a person is used to those types of actions by choice, it is wise to stop this type of action.

Correcting this type of action is important, mainly for your benefit and the benefit of your S.H.E., First you stop those actions, and if some happen to slip by, just correct them, if it is a word you said, apologize and say something good, if it is an action, also apologize and reverse it and do something good.

Actions out of habit are activities we do just because we are used to doing regardless if we need to do them or not.

Habitual actions like, drinking an extra cup of coffee that you don't want or need but purely do out of habit, eating junk food despite your knowledge that it is junk, leaving the TV on while you are asleep, the only beneficial case to leave the television on is if it is an educational program, or you are playing a video to learn something from, this way you are using your sleep time wisely, check chapter 39.

You should be aware of your wrong habitual actions, and stop them, because they do place a load on the performance of the S.H.E.

Actions on impulse are activities we do as a reaction to an action, if someone cuts us off while we are driving, we tend to retaliate without thinking, respond to something being said also without thinking, and many other examples you can discover in your actions.

Everyone is accountable for their actions, and everyone gets paid back some how, if it is a good action you have benefited your S.H.E. if it is a bad action the S.H.E. suffers as a result.

Watch what you do and correct what needs to be corrected.

External Visible Pollution

Whatever is sensed by our common five senses is classified as visible.

Hearing loud music or hearing someone screaming or shouting, or using the undesirable words, pollutes our sense of hearing.

Watching a murder on TV, or watching an immoral behavior, and unclean objects or places create a negative effect and pollutes our sense of vision.

Junk food pollutes our sense of taste as well as the other undesired effects on our health.

Smelling unpleasant odors pollutes our sense of smell.

Touching unpleasant objects, and immoral touching, pollutes our sense of touch.

Whenever our senses are polluted, that triggers an undesired effect in our system which in turn slows down the S.H.E. from its normal rate, and we become vulnerable to getting sick, depressed or simply feeling down.

This type of pollution is easily avoided as you are aware of, simply just don't do it, and don't expose yourself to whatever pollutes your senses.

External Invisible Pollution, EIP

The keyword here is invisible; meaning it is not seen, and unaware of, or used to it, to the degree that you don't feel it anymore, external invisible pollution exists everywhere, at home, at work, in the car, you name it, it has EIP, and also anything negative detected by our ultra senses, I am sure we all have the same ultra senses, with varying degrees of development.

Types of EIP are:

A - External Silent thoughts from others

B - Electromagnetic Frequencies

C - Electrical Fields

D - Magnetic Fields

E - Radio Frequency from microwave ovens

F - Vapors from wall paint, vapors from air conditioning units

G - Car exhaust

H - Buildings with tinted glass

A - External silent thought from others,

Those are quite common, they could be from friends, coworkers or people just who see us passing by in the street or in a shopping mall, or people somewhere talking bad about you, first avoid doing it yourself, and since there is no way of knowing who is doing the silent thoughts or where it is coming from, ideally you create a protective shield around you.

The protective shield can be created by visualizing yourself inside a big egg shell and have the shield filled with white or gold colors or a combination of both, then say all negative effects coming my way to stop at the shield and to be returned to their source with love and goodness.

Thinking is a natural process as we all know, even if we tell someone, why aren't you thinking, the truth is they are thinking, however their thinking is based on their knowledge and logic, not yours, don't make assumptions based on your logic alone, try to understand the other person's logic and why they talked or acted the way they did, everyone wants to be right according to their logic. Understanding helps the S.H.E. work well and you would have helped in stopping the external silent thoughts from others, and hopefully from you too.

B - Electromagnetic Frequencies, emf

For short they are termed emf, everything is composed of cells that has electrons and protons, negative and positive charges, leading to the formation of emf.

Sometimes the interaction between emf's is good, and other times it is not good, leading to the S.H.E. being affected and creation of signals to let us know that something is wrong. Signals could be, just feeling down, feeling exhausted despite the fact you haven't done anything strenuous, a muscle twitch, a sudden urge to do something, feeling sleepy after just waking up and having enough sleep, slight headache, all with the objective of letting us know something is wrong.

Electromagnetic frequency pollution affects us, because all our body functions operate on electricity in the range of millivolts, of course nothing to compare to 110 or 220 volts of the normal electricity in magnitude. Wherever there is electricity there is a magnetic field, and thus the term electromagnetic. May be for a short period of exposure the S.H.E. can handle it effectively, however long period exposure definitely has an effect. The duration of short and long are only evident by occurrence or non occurrence of symptoms, once a symptom develops that means it was long exposure even if it is one minute. Everyone's system is different in response to emf pollution. If you find a certain symptom is persistent and always occurs, check and see what is close by from computers and or television or any electronics in general; flipping channels with the remote control is a source of emf pollution, if you use the Trifield meter you will see a peak in reading as you press a button on the remote control, many times people just keep changing the television channels out of habit for an hour or so, not a good thing to do considering the amount of emf and length of exposure. The same applies to other remote control devices, like wireless mouse and keyboard of computers, as if we are not getting enough emf pollution from the computer monitor. The air is full of emf, unfortunate but it has become a way of life for many people. The amount of emf pollution is reduced by the increase in distance between you and the object emitting emf.

New cars have an abundance of electronics, which create an immense amount of emf, and is categorized as long exposure, because there is a limit to the distance that you can be away from that pollution without impairing your driving, it is in the dashboard, in the steering wheel, in the door, and a lot more places in the car.

Other interesting sources of emf are halogen and fluorescent sources of light, the latter saves on the electric bill but add a lot of emf pollution. Keep a safe distance, to be exact on what is a safe distance you need a Trifield meter, doing a search on Trifield meter on the internet will provide you with many sources if you wish to purchase one.

The electromagnetic frequency emissions have a profound effect on humans, as well as on animals and plants, keep a safe distance for your health and well being.

C – Electrical Fields

A major source of this pollution is the underground electrical cables, and wiring in the home and buildings in general, if you have a meter that detects electrical fields, use it to see the magnitude of the electrical field of the wires you have at home, when you are holding the meter close to the wire you will see a high reading, which will decrease as you go away from the source of the electrical field, this will help you know the safe distance from that wire, the S.H.E. can handle short periods of exposure, however long periods of exposure, will definitely affect your S.H.E. leading to occurrence of symptoms as warnings to you.

If you are used to having a bed lamp make sure it is at a safe distance and turned off before you sleep, as more electrical field pollution is there when you have it on. A very common occurrence is having two electrical outlets close to our bed, and on both sides of the bed, not forgetting the wiring of any devices we have plugged in, even if the device is off, the wires still emit electrical pollution, so as a rule if you don't need the device to be plugged in, unplug it, keep the plugged devices at a safe distance, and orient your bed as away as possible from electrical outlets.

Before you rent a place to live, and most definitely before buying a house to live in, you should have that type of pollution measured, you can find a lot of testing devices at this web site http://www.lessemf.com and decide either to buy or hire the services of someone who can do the testing for you.

D – Magnetic Fields

Wherever there is an electrical current regardless of its magnitude, a magnetic field is created.

Some sources of magnetic fields pollution are, improper wiring, cordless phones, remote control devices, televisions, computer monitors, electronics in cars, electric alarms and radios, even if they are off, the wires still carry electricity, and if you touch an uncovered connected wire, you will get an electrical shock. Again unplug any devices you don't need or are not using, I realize it is inconvenient to keep plugging in a device and unplugging it, but it is your well being that is at stake here, which is your most valuable asset.

To protect yourself from those magnetic fields, keep a safe distance, as effect decreases with increase in distance, and the safe distance will vary according to the device, however two feet could be safe, to be accurate you need a measuring device like a Trifield meter, check http://www.lessemf.com.

I have the Trifield meter and when I visited some friends I used it to test for magnetic fields, and to our surprise the living room which is right at the entrance of the house showed a very high reading, in comparison to the bedrooms that had zero readings, so I decided to go outside the house to try to detect where that high magnitude of magnetic field pollution is coming from, and to my amazement that high reading was the same till the middle of the street, beyond which the readings got a lot lower, so definitely the houses on the other side of the street are safer as far as magnetic pollution is concerned. I did the same testing for my house, and the results were the opposite to what was at my friend's house, so I am living on the safer side of the street.

E - Radio Frequency

Among sources of radio frequencies are cell phones and microwave ovens, with a meter you can know what you are exposed to every time you use those devices, again, keep a safe distance from such devices. For cell phones try the ones that have a speakerphone feature.

The unfortunate part of technology today are the wireless transmission towers, they are intended to have coverage everywhere, imagine when this happens, how polluted the air will be, it is not only car exhaust which comes to mind when one speaks of pollution.

F - Vapors from walls and air conditioning units

Those vapors are not healthy, despite the safe standard measures put out by various governments around the world; keep your place well aerated, even if you get some humidity and heat, it is a well worth while tradeoff. The vapor quantities are small; however they do affect our S.H.E., because they are inhaled, and it is a foreign substance, if you develop a persistent symptom, try being in a different environment and see if the symptoms disappear either right away or over time. This is one of the basic rules, always check your environment first, for example we spend a large percentage of our lives asleep probably in the same place, and once a symptom is developed, change where you sleep or change the bed orientation and observe if the symptoms disappeared, this simple change helped quite a lot of people.

G - Buildings with tinted glass

Those buildings are made that way to maintain a desired temperature; however the tinted glass prevents some sun rays and certain colors from getting into the building. The sun is there not only to provide light and warmth, but also emits very beneficial colors that are needed for the S.H.E. to work properly, like plants use the light provided by the sun for photosynthesis, and there are some plants that will not grow in the winter because of shorter days, which translates to short exposure to light, those plants need a longer day for light exposure and to absorb larger quantities of colors to complete their life cycle, the winter produce and plants get sufficient light and colors in the shorter day.

If you are in one of those buildings, make sure you go outside the building to get the benefits of the sun and light and get a full dose of all colors, at least five minutes every two to three hours, you also benefit by being away from emf emitting devices within the buildings like fluorescent lighting, fax machines, and copiers, and specially with copiers in a small room you will smell the vapor emitted and inhaled, I have seen people around copiers for a full working day, that is their job, and it is very unfortunate, because the sense of smell is adaptable, meaning you smell the vapors for a while then you don't smell them any more although they are still being emitted, you get to smell the vapors again if you go out of the room and come back or you allowed some fresh air to come in the room, and that applies to all pollution sensed by the sense of smell. I am quoting that example so that you are aware of this pollution that is visible at the beginning then becomes invisible making you think it is no longer there and you are not in danger. Just be aware of such a pollutant.

The colors are the rainbow colors ROYGBIV, red, orange, yellow, green, blue, indigo and violet. We need a balanced dose of all the colors. If a person is deprived of colors, symptoms will start occurring as a warning that something is not in harmony with our system, nothing just comes or happens to appear for no reason, there is a reason why we get headaches, a reason why we feel down, there is a always a reason for a symptom to occur.

H - Car exhaust

Car exhaust is one of the most devastating pollutants, in concentrated doses you can smell it, but normally it just is invisible, I realize there is no getting away from car exhaust, it is in the air, unless you live in the country side with bigger lots of land and less cars, where the car exhaust quantity is small in comparison to how much it is in cities. Air circulation helps dilute the effect of car exhaust, and air circulation is always better in farms and coastal areas. Non coastal cities have poor air circulation rate because of buildings blocking the natural flow of air, plus having a lot more electrical lines to provide electricity, and electrical pollution becomes an issue in cities.

Visualize with me a pond of water where a pebble is thrown into it, you will notice the formation of ripples, and before those ripples disappear another pebble is thrown close to where the first pebble was thrown, you will notice a second set of ripples forming and as this set gets wider, it intersects with the first set of ripples, breaking the ripples in the first set.

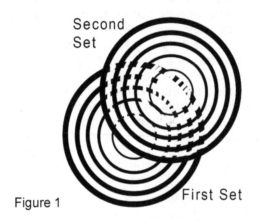

Second Set

First Set

Figure 1

The first set of ripples is like our electromagnetic field surrounding us, and the second set of ripples is like the electromagnetic field of other people or objects, the break of the first set of ripples, is like a break in our electromagnetic field, which is similar to opening a door, where interference gets in and cause symptoms to occur, anywhere in our body, and hence people get sick and the type of sickness depends on the external electromagnetic field source and strength. The normal function of the S.H.E. is impaired, and this break in electromagnetic field needs to be fixed and restored. You will know how in chapter 4 Energy Balance.

Continuous throwing of more pebbles is like continuous bombardment with electromagnetic frequencies, and here imagine what will happen to our electromagnetic field, it could be close to being obliterated.

The electromagnetic field has only one setting, which is the best setting for that person or object; whenever there is a deviation from this setting it is called a break, that needs to be fixed, you will know how to fix the breaks in chapter 4 Energy Balance.

Food additives

Chemistry and science has advanced to a great level, and many chemicals are produced synthetically, meaning produced in a factory or a laboratory from other chemicals.

There are artificial food flavors, artificial food colors, preservatives, and bleaching agents, whitening agents, and a lot more, whatever is used, unfortunately is classified as safe, personally I stay away as much as possible from foods and drinks containing such things. My kids complain all the time that I don't buy many things, I tell them when they are of legal age, they can do whatever they want, and as long as I am responsible for their well being which is now, the rule is, no drinks, no candy and no to all artificial containing food and drinks, of course if I knew earlier what I know now when my kids were younger, I wouldn't have to face this accusation, because they would have gotten older not knowing those culprits. They probably get those things at friends or relatives, but that is a small exposure, still harmful but not as much as if I had those foods and drinks at home.

The body constituents are known, and poisons are also known, however it is claimed that poison in some cases is safe like mercury which is present in flu shots.

Visit the FDA web site and do a search on mercury and flu shots, plus do another search using the words "mercury and drugs", when I did that search I was surprised to discover other medications that have mercury, for example some eye drops have mercury, remember you are always warned about fish from certain places that has a high quantity of mercury, tuna cans also have been claimed to have a percentage of mercury. So why is it allowed in medications, I have no idea, however it is interesting to read the FDA reasons, I would rather you read it for yourself, rather than me mentioning.

Do a search on the internet for medications side effects; you will be amazed at the number of returned results, read a few and know about what additives pollution do to you and your electromagnetic field and how your S.H.E. is impaired.

The intake of all those chemicals into our bodies, definitely with no doubt affects our S.H.E process.

At a younger age, one is usually tolerant to such additives, meaning the human body system can handle this pollution, but as we grow older our bodies are not as tolerant as when we are young, and the toll on our health starts to show.

To preserve the power of the normal functioning of the S.H.E. you must reduce your intake of such substances.

Another fallacy that people fall for is the diet food, and diet drinks, where the sugar is replaced by a synthetic sweetener, ask yourself which is better, sugar that is natural, or an artificial synthetic sweetener, white sugar or real brown sugar, keeping in mind that white sugar was originally brown and had to be bleached and cleaned. We get our needed sugar amounts from fruits and vegetables, by eating a well balanced menu of fruits and vegetables.

If I ever had to drink or eat something that has diet in its name, I would rather do without.

The very strange occurrence is that some of those additives are allowed in some countries and banned in other countries, although people are the same, so who is right, those who allow, or those who ban. Doing an internet search on food additives will give you a fair amount of information. I can elaborate on this specific subject; however I want you to take the initiative and take charge of your own health and get to find out things that are polluting your system and affecting your S.H.E. on your own.

Natural Pollution

Most of the natural pollution comes from underground sources in the earth. There are places where there are radioactive materials like uranium, there are quite a bit of metals, like iron, aluminum, other underground pollution comes from harmful magnetic waves, and some underground water streams intersections.

There are underground streams and wherever there is an intersection of those streams, a vortex is created, and its effects reach the surface of the earth. This type of vortex is dangerous, and most definitely must be avoided. Ancient civilizations knew about that, and that is why they were careful where they built their buildings, looking at some of the older architectural layouts, you will notice deviations from straight lines in the their fences in particular, that deviation was to avoid building on a vortex. The vortex could be located using the pendulum and then you need to clear its negative effect. Some places have been associated with certain illnesses, a major reason for those illnesses is the presence of one vortex or more, you can locate vortices as you learn how to use the pendulum as you read on and also know how to clear their effect.

Man made specific Pollution

This type of pollution is really dangerous, some are worst than others, but they are all quite dangerous to our health and our S.H.E. with multitude of symptoms being created.

A type of this pollution that has been addressed by some countries is waste disposal of chemicals into rivers and water streams, and to some extent chemical gases, I say some extent, because gases are mostly invisible, and don't have an immediate impact to be felt by inhabitants of those areas. To even a lesser extent fine powders coming out of the stacks of some industries.

The skies at the levels from a few thousand to 40,000 feet or more away from earth are full of pollution, on one of my trips by plane I noticed an airplane going in the opposite direction and have seen the amount of dark exhaust coming out of it, I never realized this pollution until I saw it with my own eyes. This type of exhaust is moved by winds and air currents to various places around the world, until they are brought down to earth by rain, and how can we know who is to blame. Space shuttles even create more pollution than airplanes, just watch a launch of one of those space shuttles and you will realize how much of an effect this is causing, not to mention the pollution at even higher levels than airplanes.

Another type of man made pollution which has a long lasting effect is nuclear waste from nuclear facilities; some might remember the Russian Chernobyl nuclear incident which affected many countries. Initially that type of nuclear waste was buried deep underground and in the deep oceans, unfortunately the containers of this waste started to leak, affecting the earths' underground levels and oceans, with a definite effect on the S.H.E. of the earth and the oceans and all life forms that cam in contact with that radioactive pollution.

Nuclear testing carried out underground and under water has really devastating effects, a most recent effect could be the Asian Tsunami, and it could have resulted from neighboring nuclear testing or the Chinese nuclear testing. The earth is affected by those high powered nuclear explosions, and the pressure waves created keep on propagating in all directions, affecting the earths' layers, including oceans and rivers.

This latter type is still going on to this day, where, when and how, is a puzzle, although it isn't a puzzle to those involved in making nuclear testing. Earthquakes and shaking of the earth will continue to occur in new places that are not characterized as being in earthquake zones, with the larger S.H.E. being affected, causing numerous effects on plants and animals life and definitely on humans.

Other types of Pollution

Most of the types of pollution mentioned above are man made, and if the trend continues, a lot more types will be created, with many more types of diseases and syndromes occurring, syndromes are usually a collection of symptoms, and those latest diseases and syndromes will have the name of the discoverer listing all the symptoms and probable causes, however the real root of the disease is of unknown origin.

The S.H.E. and the master cell warn us by giving us signals that something is wrong, from any of those pollution types. The signal could be in a form of a symptom like a headache, a muscle ache, a rash; it could be a multitude of occurrences coming from the commonly known conscious senses as well as other signals from the ultra-conscious.

You will reap great rewards for yourself by being aware of those types of pollution, and avoiding them, and protecting yourselves and your loved ones. With the ultimate effect of having a normally functioning S.H.E..

Chapter 3

Restoration of the Electromagnetic Field

To restore the electromagnetic field, we must acknowledge the following:

Be aware that we have a unique high power Self Healing Energy.

Clean our surroundings as mentioned in the pollution chapter.

By cleaning the surroundings and clearing a lot of the pollution, you have just removed a cause that makes imbalance in our electromagnetic field, which if not corrected will cause many symptoms leading to disease, and even when you get better, you will get sick again.

However removing the cause, doesn't mean that the imbalance will be restored immediately, and here there are several methods with which you can make restoration faster.

Energy Balance is the method I use the most, why, because it is a personal preference, and you will have your preferences as you read along and practice the different methods. I find myself incorporating all the different methods differently in different situations.

Once you know about the different methods, you will come to the conclusion that you prefer one method; however you will also find yourself incorporating all methods into one method of your own.

Some people will prefer one method over another, some will come up with their own method, and some will use different methods for different situations.

At this stage don't be concerned with which method you will choose, avoid preconceptions, and become familiar and knowledgeable about the methods in this book, and you could read other books explaining other methods that might interest you as well, and you will find yourself choosing a method without even realizing it.

The other methods I incorporate into how I help people are, Color Balance, Relaxology, Listenology, Hypnosis, Line Body Parts Balance, plus my own intuition that has been proven to be right in many cases.

Chapter 4

Energy Balance

Energy can neither be created nor destroyed, but it can be balanced and directed.

Four years ago I had the fortune – at the end you will know why I say fortune - of having a foot pain, so I did what everyone does went to the family doctor, who ordered x-rays, and examined my foot then I was referred to another doctor.

I went to the other doctor who explained a lot of issues regarding my foot, and about the condition and why and how to fix it, the suggestions were that I place an insert in the shoe to relieve the tension off the muscles, otherwise I will end up with a more serious condition, anyway, I was not happy with that specially that the insert would cost over $200 and this wasn't covered by insurance.

I then went to where I used to work at the time and mentioned what happened with my foot condition to a colleague of mine, Vince Kaye, who offered to help and clear the condition, of course I said go ahead, and within seconds I felt heat going through my foot and the pain was gone, I was amazed of how quick the relief was and even more astonished that this even took place within seconds and without being touched and without medications.

I was very intrigued and asked Vince if he would teach me how to do what he did, he said, yes, and he called what he did, Energy Balance.

The next week-end we met for the first lesson.

Vince told me earlier to get a pendulum which I did from http://www.intuitivedowsing.com and I bought the brass ball pendulum, at this stage any pendulum would do.

The first lesson was to have the following colors available:

Red – Blue – Green – Yellow – Gold

Then use the pendulum to know at what length it will go clockwise, the pendulum is made up of a string and the ball, see figure 2, you hold the string close to the ball and the rest of the string inside your palm as in figure 3, then hold the pendulum above the color red and start letting the string loose slowly until it rotates clockwise as in figure 4, and this becomes the point where the pendulum responds for red. Repeat the same process for the remainder of the colors.

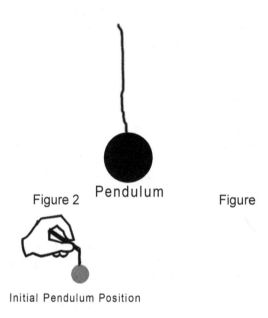

Figure 2   Pendulum   Figure

Initial Pendulum Position

3

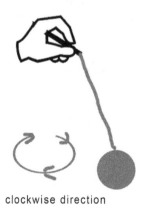

clockwise direction

Figure 4

An easy way to have colors is to use index cards and colored dots which are both available at most stationary stores, use one dot per index card, and you will have five index cards, each having a dot of a different color.

This first lesson took me over a week to get done, and just before I succeeded I almost gave up as the pendulum just wouldn't rotate. It was quite frustrating not being able to do it, and after I managed to do it, it was just a great feeling of success, never even thought why it took so long, it worked and I was happy.

During the process of trying to get the pendulum to rotate, I told Vince several times, the pendulum doesn't want to move, and asked so many questions, however he wouldn't offer any more help, and said just keep trying, it will, and he was right, the reason I am mentioning that, is I don't want you to give up, as for some people it might be done in a shorter period and for others it might take longer.

To help in getting the pendulum to move to various frequencies of color, practice deep breathing, and that helps reduce the clutter of thoughts in the mind, and allows you to reach an alpha state, at the alpha state the brain waves are at a lower rate than the conscious state, perform the deep breathing before using the pendulum, to reach the alpha state of mind. A most common question that I am asked is, how many times should deep breathing be done or how much time it takes to reach the alpha state, and my reply always is, there is no set numbers for breathing and no set amount of time to reach the alpha state, you will know it once you get to it, as I mentioned earlier it took me more than a week to reach the alpha state, of course I didn't do deep breathing for the whole period, it was an on and off situation, where I practice, and then stop for a while then start again and so on for the whole period until the pendulum moved, and that was how I knew I reached the alpha state. Reaching the alpha state once for the first time is really all you need, as afterwards it is a lot easier and could be reached within minutes or seconds, now I am at the stage of reaching alpha state at will, meaning whenever I want, and you will achieve the same result as I did. This was also introduced to me by Vince.

A good introduction to pendulums is available at this web site http://www.lettertorobin.org

Now it is time for the second lesson with Vince, I was looking forward to that second lesson, feeling great that I succeeded in getting the pendulum to move and being able to reach the alpha state.

Vince started explaining that everything, every entity has its own unique frequency or vibration the same as colors had their own frequency, Vince continued on to explain about breaks which are an interruption to normal happenings or normal flow in a process, and that all entities have an energy field which could be called an electromagnetic field, and a break always refers to a break in the electromagnetic field or energy field, and the break could be associated with symptoms, and in many cases the break is present or already took place before the symptoms occur, at this stage the type of symptom is not important, and we should be concerned with identifying where the break is. To know where the break is in the energy field of a person, we just write the name of the person on a piece of paper or an index card, and use the pendulum until it rotates clockwise at that person's frequency the same way we did with the colors, most pendulums have a type of a marker that can be moved up and down the string, now move the marker to that point in the string at which it rotated clockwise identifying the person's frequency, see figure 5, then get an anatomy book and a pointing object which could be a pen or pencil.

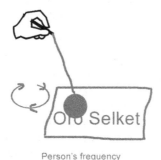

Person's frequency

Figure 5

Now you have established the frequency of the person, hold the pendulum at that frequency over the person's name, an indication that you are at the right frequency is that the pendulum will rotate clockwise once it is over the name, and then hold the pointing device with the other hand over one of the pages of the anatomy book, and move the pointing device to various spots in the diagram, if there is a break in the energy field of that person the pendulum will rotate anticlockwise at where the break is.

I usually use this figure as in figure 6, to identify the breaks, and if I want more details I use the anatomy book for the relevant area already identified from figure 6.

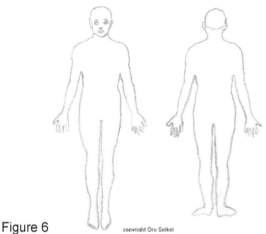

Figure 6

Which hand should be used to hold the pendulum, this is a personal choice, just do it as it comes naturally to you. Regarding the pointing device, if you use a pen or pencil, make sure you don't leave marks on the paper or book, unless you intentionally want to do that, or use a pointer that will not leave marks.

Now you have located where the break is, all you have to do now is keep the pointing device pointing to that area and force the pendulum to rotate clockwise, and maintain that clockwise motion for some time, while you are at the alpha state, and at the same time project with your mind the color gold to that break, how long, you will know when it is done.

Then continue scanning the diagram in the anatomy book looking for other breaks in the energy field, and do as we did with the first break in the energy field.

Then go back with the pointing device to the first spot that had the break and see how the pendulum rotates, if it is clockwise then it is fixed, if the pendulum rotates anti clockwise, repeat the process again of forcing the pendulum to rotate clockwise. In most cases once the break is fixed the symptom disappears, if it was there to start with, remember that sometimes the break appears before a symptom occurs, and by fixing the break the symptom that was going to appear at some stage will not manifest itself. If you regularly check your energy field and fix breaks as you find them, you will not have symptoms occurring. The regular checking will become easier as you do energy balanced advanced.

Before you attempt to fix the breaks in the energy field of someone else you must get the permission of the person first, if you are doing energy balance to minors get their parents or guardians permission.

In some cases the break will not get fixed, and it could be one of several reasons:

> 1 – The permission is not true, meaning the person just said so to be courteous but didn't really mean it.

> 2 – The cause of the break in energy field is still there and whenever you fix it, it gets broken again, and it could be the presence of one of the pollution items we discussed earlier.

> 3 – The higher wisdom which I call God, decides it is better for the person not to fix the break at this particular time.

> 4 – It is not beneficial to the client to get rid of the symptom associated with the break in energy field, as the symptom is a signal for something more serious that needs attending to, and if pain goes away, the major issue could be ignored.

There are limitations, the same way there are limitations to any method, nothing is ever absolute except God.

Please read the article that Vince and I wrote jointly;

Energy Balancing Concepts

By Vince Kaye, Remote Energy Balancer

and

Oro Selket, Remote Energy Balancer, Listenologist

Our Electrical Nature

Some individuals enjoy long lives and robust health. These individuals seem to bounce back quickly from illness or injury, while others seem to require a long time and a great deal of care to recover. We attribute the differences between the healthy and the less-than-healthy individuals to various combinations of genes, nutrition, life style, and "luck". While each of these reasons seems to explain many of the differences between the two groups, there always seem to be the exceptions that cannot be explained.

A clue to those with exceptional health is our electrical natures. Our bodies run on electricity, and if that electrical flow is cut off or impeded, then significant effects may result, from paralysis, as in a severe spinal injury, to numbness or pain in an extremity, as in a pinched or damaged nerve. The Eastern practice of acupuncture uses needles inserted at specific points in order to promote, enhance, and maintain the flow of energy, or "chi", within the body. This energy flow then appears to bring benefit to the individual. The electrical flow between these points can be measured with sensitive electronic instruments, which show a change in the electrical flow before and after the application of the needles.

Each of us is surrounded by an electromagnetic field that cannot be perceived by most people. If that field is impeded or interrupted, then we may experience negative effects such as illness, pain, insomnia, or an extended recuperative interval. We can impede or interrupt our field as a result of a long-forgotten injury, a major surgical procedure, or a minor tap to an acupuncture point. Because modern technology pays little attention to the field that surrounds each of us, the energy flow's importance to our health or recuperative capability is not considered.

In this article, we will discuss how we have brought apparent benefit to individuals by balancing their energy fields and illustrate it with some of the anecdotal results of our work.

BioEnergy Concepts

Each cell in our bodies is a miniature chemical factory in which many thousands of complex life-sustaining reactions occur each second. Each chemical reaction involves the transfer or movement of electrons between molecules and atoms. The movement of electrons gives rise to minute electrical currents and hence we are electro-chemical beings. In a sense, each cell is a microscopic battery.

Our bodies require electrical energy to operate. Electrical signals within the brain and between the brain and various bodily systems sustain our lives. The electrical connection between our brain and heart is essential for life. The cells and the numerous electrical pathways within the body generate the electromagnetic field that surrounds each of us.

The body's electromagnetic field seems to have a very powerful effect on the body's operations. For example, many individuals can be trained to do "hands-on" therapeutic touch. Sensitive instruments have shown that the trained individual applying the therapeutic touch emits a pulsing magnetic field that a subject's field picks up, or resonates with, to produce benefit for the subject.

Frequencies

The electrical energies that help to run our bodily functions have associated frequencies that contain information about our health. Qualified personnel can analyze the frequencies associated with the brain (EEG) and the heart (EKG) to identify abnormal behaviors in those organs.

Each of us has a unique frequency because of our unique genetic profile. Biochemists use DNA analysis to identify the specific individual from whom a bit of hair, blood, saliva, skin, etc has been obtained. DNA analysis allows us to positively identify one's ancestors through a lineage that spans hundreds of generations.

In effect, we all transmit information about our physical and psychological states, much like a radio or television station broadcasts information. Although the strength of our broadcast signal is weak in comparison to a radio or television signal, our transmissions can be detected and analyzed to identify and correct imbalances in our energy fields.

Resonance

Frequencies may be measured and affected through a principle called resonance. Radios and televisions operate by tuning a circuit to the frequency of a desired signal and amplifying the detected signal. The detecting circuit is said to be tuned to the resonant frequency.

We constantly broadcast information about our health and psychological state. Everyone has experienced the presence of individuals who almost instantly make us feel secure, heard, welcome, or respected. We have also been in the presence of individuals who make us feel anxious, fearful, depressed or angry. We refer to individuals as having good or bad "vibes" – and this is much more than a figure of speech. We are, in fact, tuning in, or resonating, with these individuals' frequencies.

Our memories also contain the frequencies that are associated with the objects of our memories. We can recall the name of an individual who we have not seen or spoken with for some time, and associate a feeling with that individual. Or we can think of a happy individual, and our mind will supply us with the images of individuals who we remember as being happy.

Using Resonance

Just as it is possible for an individual to affect those in his or her immediate vicinity through his or her psychological state, it is possible for those around that individual to affect the individual through their psychological states. Consider the power of prayer: Numerous studies have shown that surgical patients who are prayed for are more likely to have shorter recuperation times than those who are not the objects of prayer. And the patients who are prayed for need not be aware that they are being prayed for!

The power of prayer may operate through the resonance principle. Those doing the praying are holding the individual in mind while visualizing, in whatever way they can, the individual's rapid recovery. The image of the individual is in resonance with the individual himself or herself, and the individual thus receives the benefits of the prayers.

This is the way in which remote energy balancing operates: The individual doing the energy balancing holds the subject's frequency and an intention in mind simultaneously. The energy balancer, the subject, and the intention are all in resonance, and the subject and the balancer receive the same benefit.

Each being and object emits a characteristic frequency, which is subject to resonance principles. In addition, each emotion, belief, and thought has a characteristic frequency. Therefore, it is possible to affect an energy field – both the physical and psychological – at a distance and bring benefit to the individual by 'repairing' energy impediments or breaks in the individual or object's energy field. We can do that by working on a mental 'model' of the subject's energy field. The subject may experience the benefits of the balance that we bring to the model. Generally, remote energy balancing requires only seconds or a few minutes at most. Time and space do not seem to matter in a remote energy balancing session.

We worked on the energy field of a 55 year old man who underwent a major surgical operation shortly after the procedure. Although the standard hospital stay is 72 hours for the procedure, he was discharged within 24 hours after the surgery since he required no pain-killing medication. We identified an energy break at the site of the surgery and 'repaired' the break to allow the flow of energy that apparently speeded his recuperation. As of this writing, his surgeon reports that his recuperation is about four months ahead of expectations.

In April 2001, we balanced the energy field in the sinus area of an individual with pollen and animal-dander allergies. He felt a benefit within 90 minutes and the condition has never returned. He remains unaffected by the high pollen counts of spring and can now be in a symptom-free presence of cats, which once caused him great sinus discomfort. Apparently, the break in the man's energy field led to his sinus problems and the repair of the energy break has allowed him to become free of sinus problems.

Remote energy balancing can also bring benefit to animals because they are also surrounded by electromagnetic fields. We remotely balanced a cat's energy field that suffered from an upset stomach. The cat was observed eating normally soon afterwards.

Each of our energy fields seems to protect us from detrimental energies. The protective energy field is the energetic analog to our physical immune system. An energy balancer who intends to send detrimental energy to a subject will find it very difficult to influence the subject negatively, and the balancer will experience the detrimental effects of the intention. Therefore, the worst that can happen to the subject is – nothing, but the person sending the negative energies will be adversely affected!

Energy Balancing Limitations

We have reports from individuals who have described benefits with allergies, anxiety, toothaches, back and neck pain, and joint pain. We have worked with teachers, nurses, engineers, managers, and executives. Each of these individuals used our services in conjunction that they were receiving from qualified physicians, therapists, and other health-care professionals. We have also worked with instructors to remotely balance their classrooms to promote an environment that is conducive to learning

Because we are electro-chemical and electro-mechanical beings, we need the attention and care of qualified health-care professionals as well. Remote energy balancing can be a useful addition to a health-care professional's recommended treatment, and must not be used as a substitute for the recommended treatment.

Does energy balancing work in all cases? The answer is no. Like all tools and techniques, there are no guarantees and sometimes the subject experiences no benefit. We are continuing our research into why the technique does not work in these cases. However, we are mindful of the fact that there are questions for which there may be no apparent solutions.

Additional Information

You can visit web site at:

http://www.OroSelket.com.

Vgkubilus@hotmail.com use subject SHE

The next recommendation to me from Vince was to read the book Energy Medicine by Donna Eden, which proved to be quite valuable, it has meridian diagrams for many organs of the body, and you can also use Line body diagrams as in chapter 13.

The meridians are certain paths within our body that govern certain organs, like the kidney, the heart, the stomach and other organs.

At the same time I was reading the book Energy Medicine, a very close friend of mine who is a physician was suffering from kidney stones, I asked his permission to do energy balance and because of the pain the kidney stones causes he said please do, despite the fact as a physician he was skeptic to what I do.

I used the kidney meridian in the Energy Medicine book and the pendulum and found the location of the breaks in the kidney meridian and immediately forced the pendulum to go clockwise to fix the breaks.

The kidney stones were showing in the tests made and weren't responding to medication, so my friend decided to go and have surgery to remove the stones, that day was very memorable; because after the surgery the doctor came and said he didn't find any stones, I knew that my energy balance work has brought benefit to my friend, and I was very pleased and amazed at the same time, my friend of course being skeptic said they dissolved, I said if they did why did you have surgery, I didn't want to discuss the issue further, as it serves no purpose, I don't want credit to satisfy the ego, so I simply said, just be aware that there alternative means to the traditional medicine.

It is ironical that we say traditional medicine and it is less than a hundred years old, and that we say alternative medicine about methods that have been used for thousands of years by the Pharos and the Chinese; and withstood the test of time, alternative medicine is very powerful and very useful, and alternative medicine probably has helped more people through the thousands of years than the number of people helped by traditional medicine.

Research today is a business, and the companies that offer money for research want favorable results, they want a positive return on investment, and if any researcher dares to do things differently they will never get any more money for research. Visit the FDA web site and search for an article that has research money, and you will find out for yourself what I mean.

Research standards has been set by the same people who do the research for those who will benefit by the research, with regards to research for alternative medicine, no one has this kind of money to do that magnitude of research.

After a few months, a friend of mine in another country who also had a kidney stone, but this was a large one as told to him by his doctor, and the doctor said that surgery is a must, I asked my friend for permission and one week, after I was granted permission I started working on the energy breaks I found in the kidney meridian and within one week the stone was gone, to the amazement of my friend and the total disbelief of his doctor.

Another quite amazing case was of a friend of mine who is a physician, he had two sons who suffered from thirty kidney stones every week, and there is the content of his testimonial: I have changed the names.

"My son john was admitted to the hospital for 6 weeks last year, for kidney stones which blocked both of his kidneys. We had Lithotrypsy done (Lazer destruction of kidney stones) in addition to many other procedures to avoid surgery and to save both kidneys. Soon after John was sent home, my other son, David, started passing about 30 stones a week.

We really panicked. Our nephrologist was puzzled because we had tried every conceivable medicine and medical technique that we could. Finally she determined that we had to just handle the kidney stones as they formed. The outlook was that we were going to spend a lot of time in hospitals, until their kidneys fail.

Both my boys have a rare disability (Lesch-Nyhan Syndrome) where kidney failure is a sure thing, eventually. Unlike any other kidney disease, the stones occur in the kidney tissue then pass to the urine passages. If they stay within the kidney tissue they damage it and reduce kidney functions. If they are small enough and pass down with urine they cause excrusciating renal colics. But, usually they are too big to pass down and we often have to deal with blocked kidneys in the emergency room. Kidney stones forming both in the kidney tissue and in the urine passages eventually cause the kidneys to fail at a young age. In addition to the miseries of their disability itself, they have to perform dialysis from then on.

In January, Oro called me to offer his Oroselket Methods. Though skeptical, I trusted him enough to agree.

Now, in March, I'm in disbelief that both boys stopped passing stones in urine. X-ray images of the kidneys do not show stones in the urine passages at all. And stones in the kidney tissues remain the same (not getting bigger).

I am stunned.

I am myself a physician and I cannot think of any logical explanation but to conclude that Oro's Oroselket method works.

It does

We have not given John and David any medications that are different from those that they had been taking for a year and a half before John was admitted to the hospital last year. The nephrologist and I had both determined that there was nothing we could do but deal with stones as they form. And, we expected kidney stones to keep forming.

Strangely enough, 3 months after Oro's Oroselket Methods, John and David's kidneys have been back to their basics, continuously. Even if it turns out to be temporary, a full 3 month of relief is a miracle we could not hope to happen, otherwise.

There is truth about Oroselket. Strange name for a wonderful cure.

Thank you, Oro. From the bottom of my heart.

You can add this letter as an endorsement for Oroselket on your web site.

Abraham"

Remember what I mentioned earlier about thought pollution and having the wrong thoughts or saying the wrong things, notice the statement in my friend's testimonial:

"Strangely enough, 3 months after Oro's Oroselket Methods, John and David's kidneys have been back to their basics, continuously. Even if it turns out to be temporary, a full 3 month of relief is a miracle we could not hope to happen, otherwise."

His permission was for 3 months, he said it unknowingly, and strangely enough the kids started having kidney stones again.

Be very careful what you say, it affects you in more ways than you can even imagine.

Several months have passed and I use the pendulum and the anatomy book and the meridians successfully, until Vince told me that we can do energy balance without the pendulum and the anatomy book, and instead; use our minds to perform the same procedure, so I started doing the procedure in my mind as if the pendulum and books are there, and to my amazement, the results were astounding, that case was a breast cyst for a lady friend I knew, one week later she had a mammogram done and the cyst is gone, for women, having a breast cyst is very scary, as it might be cancerous.

To me that was quite an accomplishment, to do the work using my mind with no pendulum and no books. Check chapter 5 Energy Balance Advanced

The mind is very powerful and it will do whatever you command it to do, and since then most of my energy balance work has been done mentally, and in some cases I revert to the use of the pendulum and the anatomy book, two good anatomy books that I use are

- Atlas of the Human Body by Takeo Takahashi

- Human Body An illustrated guide to every part of the human body and how it works

Other cases that have been helped successfully using the same methods are

Back pains

Glaucoma

Knee pains

Arthritis

Gout

Cancer

Elbow pains

Migraine headaches

Carper tunnel

Bladder infections

Ear infections

Shoulder pains

As a rule we should always be in good health, however our thoughts and the external pollution we are exposed to affect us. Whenever there is pain it is like a stop sign we should stop and look to see what went wrong and fix the situation.

Another rule, when we wake up in the morning we should be well rested and feeling good, if that is not the case, then we have to check what we have been exposed to the night before, what did we eat, what addition did we have in the bedroom, did we leave the TV on all night.

Energy Balance is one of the methods to fix our electromagnetic field or energy field and allow the S.H.E. to work perfectly.

Chapter 5

Energy Balance Advanced

The start of Energy Balance was using the pendulum and the anatomy book and the meridians, next was using the same tools but instead used the mind without the physical use of the pendulum and books, as taught by my friend and teacher Vince Kaye.

The next step was using the mind to actually find where the break in the electromagnetic field is and fixing it. I tell myself I want to see where the break is and when I am shown where the break is, I reach the alpha stage and project gold into the break using the mind, and this has been done with great success, do what you did with the pendulum but with your mind and pretend that the pendulum is in your hand, and mentally rotate it clockwise over the break in the electromagnetic field or energy field, and you can definitely get to the alpha stage quicker, and ask to be shown where the break is and you will amazed when you immediately see with your mind where the break is. There are no limitations; if limitations exist it is because you imposed them.

One time I had a client who had glaucoma and knee problems, I sent energy to the knee, and the client immediately felt the relief and the pain was gone, and then I started sending energy to the eyes, but no effect, then I asked to myself where is the cause of the problem and I was shown the break in the electromagnetic field at the right side around the kidney area and I sent energy there and the eye was relieved, and I met the client at a function, three months later and asked her how is she doing, she said great and the knee and the glaucoma conditions are gone and never came back. This is an example where the break could be in a different area from where the actual symptom is.

One question I am always asked by clients, should I stop the medication, and my reply is always consult your physician. Never play doctor.

There are no limits to what you can do, the only limits is what you impose on yourself, so be careful, you have been shown how I started, how I progressed, and you can do the same to make the S.H.E. work better for you and others.

A client contacted me over the phone, requesting my help in a condition in the stomach, so I did the energy balance and she was relieved of her pain, however the pain and symptom kept on coming back, and I did energy balance again, and she was relieved, however the pain keeps coming back, this kept on happening for a week.

Then we talked again, and as we are talking I discovered that the reason the pain and symptom kept coming back was internal thought pollution, she has told herself that once she gets better she will start business again, however because of her earlier painful experience with the business, her subconscious thoughts were to protect her from a repeat of that pain, and the stomach pain was the way for her protection, so was the internal thought pollution, once I told her that, she realized how her mind was controlling her, and she changed her thought process and told herself, that starting business again will cause no pain, her stomach pain was gone.

Analyzing the above case, you will find out that the mind caused all this pain, for protection from a bigger pain, so it thought, and once the thought process was changed, all went back to normal and the S.H.E. worked normally and is ready for any more work that is beneficial to the individual, this also is a Listenology example. Chapter 16 Listenology

Every individual has the perfect solution to their problems.

We are born and exposed to many variables through our parents, grandparents, and all whom we get in contact with, plus what we hear from television, radio, what we get exposed to in schools, in reality anything that touches our senses either at the conscious level or at the ultra-conscious level affects us from the day of our inception, a baby cannot talk back, however it is all stored in the mind, good or bad is stored in the mind to come out at a later age.

That exposure shapes our future thoughts and affect how we think and behave, even if we don't remember those incidences, and no one but you has this knowledge and many times you don't realize you have them, how many times did you tell yourself "how did I do that" you might not have an answer, but the answer lies in what you have been exposed to as a child, or even as an adult.

Your mind and your body all work in harmony to bring you the best of everything, but it is the internal thought pollution that keeps you back.

We are born and even since inception we are good, it is the external pollution that shapes our habits, shapes our actions and shapes our future, once you realize that, then you are back to your good self, unless you decide to remain as before, it is all within your power and within your capabilities.

That is why I say no one has a better solution to your problem than you.

One of the reasons the solution doesn't come to mind immediately, is because we have so many things we interact with and that we have developed routine actions to almost every situation, for example, when we get in the car, we always do the same exact thing every time, when we wake up in the morning we always get out of bed the same way, and probably do things automatically for thirty minutes, from washing our face to getting a shower to having coffee or tea or breakfast to turning the TV on.

When we want to sit on the couch, we do it the same exact way every time, when we go to bed we also do it the same way, and create the same environment night after night without even thinking.

When we go to the kitchen, we have certain things we do the same way, watch yourself and you will realize how many things we do automatically, even arguments between spouses, it boils down to the same issue every time.

Why do we do that, because the mind follows the path of least work, and it is a lot easier to do the same thing than come up with something different, it is easier to live with the problem than to think of a solution so does the mind thinks.

To make the solution to your problem come out and be known to you, you first must realize that you have the solution, and that your mind and all your systems work for your benefit, and start looking at things from a broader scope and from the outside, how many times are you able to advise others and when it comes to you in similar situations you feel helpless, how many times did you say "I knew it" after talking with someone. The key is looking at situations from the outside.

The reason you are able to help others and many times say "I knew it" is because you looked at issues from the outside, imagine you are in a circle with all your family and work interactions, to find the solution all you have to do is step out of this imaginary circle that your mind placed you in, see chapter 16 for more details on Listenology.

Reread the above stated facts, and practice a few times, and you will definitely be able to perform advanced energy balance in an easier manner. Be assured it is quite simple and all you need is your desire.

Now you know how to perform energy balance advanced, using your mind, and now you can do daily check ups for you and your family and whoever grants you permission.

An important concept is demonstrated in the above examples, which is, you can do energy balance remotely, meaning you don't need the physical presence of the person, all that is needed is the permission of the person to energy balance their energy field. Performing remote energy balance also applies to all the coming chapters as well.

Chapter 6

Energy Balance for Places

This concept and how it is handled was also introduced to me by Vince Kaye.

Places, like home, work, meeting rooms, or any place for that matter, are affected by what happens in it, I am sure you have experienced getting into a place and feeling very comfortable and getting into other places where you feel terrible and just want to get out.

Whenever we feel happiness, we project it into the place where we are and the energy in the place is energy of happiness.

Whenever sadness or quarrels or trouble happens in a place, that also is projected in the place and the energy is sad energy, the wrong television show will also project its negative energy.

The energy projected in a place remains in the place until it is cleared, or replaced by another type of energy, some people that are more sensitive pick up on those energies more than others, this is what some people call vibes.

The same way we have done energy balance with the pendulum, anatomy book and meridians, we can also balance a place, using the pendulum and a sketch of the place, and whenever the pendulum rotates anticlockwise, you can force the pendulum to rotate clockwise and project gold color to balance the place energetically, here you also need the permission of the person responsible for the place at that particular time. For example if I was to balance a meeting room, I would require the permission of the person administering the meeting or the permission of the person who the meeting is about.

I can perform the energy balancing of a place using my mind, and you can do the same, it is all a matter of what you believe you can do. The same way I request to myself to see where the break in energy in a human body, I do the same for places and request to see or be shown where the break is, and then once the break in the energy field of the place is identified, I am able to fix the break, visualizing a very big pendulum over the place and rotate it clockwise and project gold into the place.

To be present in a well balanced place is definitely a plus for our health and sanity. Balancing a place before an important meeting is very helpful, and promotes fairness and ethical behavior.

One time I had a friend running an adult computer class, and he had a problem in keeping the class quiet, so he asked for my help, I asked for permission, and he granted me the permission, within one minute the whole class was quiet and were listening to the lesson being taught, the place was balanced for four days, as this is what I thought the length of the course was, however my friend contacted me again on the fifth day asking for help again, I said I thought the class is only four days, he said no it is a week long, so I balanced the place for the remaining period and things went very well. What I did, was to project gold in a clockwise direction filling the whole place.

Another case, was a client who is a high school teacher, in an urban area, who had incredible problems with the students, they just wouldn't stop being disruptive and rude, I was asked for help, and after I got the permission, I balanced the place, the same way by projecting gold in a clockwise direction and the feedback I got later was; the students were immediately quiet and the class went on in a good way.

Balancing the place, makes everyone in that place revert to their normal good self, as mentioned earlier we are born good, and it is the internal and external visible and invisible pollution that affect us, so when the place is balanced, the pollution effect in that place at that time is non existent.

I had another client, who was worried about her son who was charged with trespassing, and court date was set, in a court known by its prejudices or very strict enforcement of the law, as she was told by the lawyer. She granted me permission and told me the date and time, so I immediately started balancing the place, and for some unknown reason to me the place just didn't want to get balanced, I am quoting this example to show that you do get immediate feedback if the energy sent has reached its destination or not, so I said to myself I will try later. The next day I received a call from the client informing me that the date and time were changed, and then I knew why the place wouldn't get balanced earlier, I was given the new date and time and this time the place responded to my attempts and was balanced.

Later, the client called me to thank me for the work I have done, and told me, all went better than expected as said to her by her lawyer, they didn't believe themselves with the results, and her son got the minimum possible judgment, under the law.

As mentioned earlier balancing a place makes everyone in the place revert to their good self, and no prejudices plus keeping all pollution effects away from the place.

Nature also has its effects on us; there are many factors, all those metals and ores and oil and streams of water, and even radioactive materials all underground, have their effect on us, people of earlier civilizations knew about those spots and avoided building in those areas.

That is why the negative energy, whatever its source, it needs to be identified and cleared, and or provide the protective measures against their effects.

As mentioned earlier, you can locate the break in the energy field of the place, regardless of its source, and use the pendulum and force it to rotate clockwise while projecting gold into the place or you can use your mind and project gold in a clockwise manner. If there are more breaks in the place, just repeat the same process of projecting gold to those other breaks as well.

To protect the place against future breaks in the energy field, you can place a protective shield around the place, and fill the shield with gold color; the shape of the protective shield can be any shape you feel would get the place protected, however, the eggshell shape is easy to project and easy to fill with gold, and that is my preferred shape for protective shields.

Another client, had a problem with her husband, and complained to me that her husband always starts up arguing and quarreling for no apparent reason, I asked for permission to balance their home, permission was granted and I balanced the home, and two days later I receive a call from her, thanking me and telling me that her husband changed completely and all was well.

I had another client who had four tumors in one lung, and they were of the malignant type, I got her permission to do energy balance for her and for her home, and I did energy balance for her and also for the home. A week later I received a call from her thanking me for what I did, and she told me that she was very skeptic, however her condition is incredibly better and she felt great for the first time in many years since she got the tumors, she told me despite her feeling skeptic, she told herself she has nothing to lose but my fees, but now she is very grateful and happy that she spent that money for her well being.

The above case illustrates the value of energy balance for humans and places for the same person. Usually with cancer clients the place where they live must be balanced as well, because there is a high possibility of the place being the cause of the cancer, there has been numerous studies where people who live in certain areas get similar diseases, the same with people who live close to power lines, here is not the place to go through those studies, however doing a search on the internet will provide you with a lot more information.

Chapter 7

Energy Balance for Animals and Birds

Energy balance for animals is done the same way as it is done to humans, using the pendulum and anatomy charts.

However once you reach the stage of doing the energy balance using your mind it would be easier to work on animals, because you will not need the anatomy books, and animal's anatomy is different from one species to another, unless you specialize in one or two animals and get their anatomy books.

I have done energy balance on dogs, cats and horses, with great success, provided I had their owner's permission.

One of the ways that you can use to do energy balance on animals using a pendulum, is to draw a sketch of the animal, head including eyes, ears, jaw, and neck, then the body and here you can write the organs names, then the legs and tail.

For birds you do a sketch as well with the main outline.

Or you can do a search for example for dog or canine anatomy, and find a web site like this one here http://www.lowchensaustralia.com/health/anatomy.htm, or for feline anatomy, or horse anatomy, and you will find many images that will help you identify the various organs in an animal or a bird.

One client I had, reported to me that her horse is not normal and not eating as usual and looks down, after her permission I started my work and located the energy breaks in the energy field of the horse and fixed them, and the following week I received a thank you call.

Here I used energy balance advanced using my mind, and located where the break is, and projected gold in a clockwise direction to the spot where the break in the energy field is. This is another example of performing remote energy balance.

Most of my work is for humans, although the same principle of finding the break in the electromagnetic field or energy field and fixing it applies.

Many people have pets, and that is a very good way of helping their pets overcome the discomfort. Animals and birds are also affected by some of the pollution types mentioned in chapter 2, and there could be more pollution or different types of pollution that we are not aware of, energy balance will definitely be of great help.

Chapter 8

Energy Balance for Plants and Trees

The vegetation world is an integral part of our life; it provides oxygen and takes away carbon dioxide, and we couldn't live without it, and it is food for us, and paper and furniture are made from trees.

A plant has its own world and surroundings; it is affected by everything around it.

Pollution is also a factor affecting the S.H.E. of the vegetation world, including plants and trees.

The same way we did energy balance on humans and animals, we do the same for a plant or tree, using a pendulum and a drawing or sketch of the object, or use the mind, whichever you are comfortable doing.

Another aspect that is quite important for the growth of the plant or tree is its making use of all the surroundings energies to its benefit.

Examples of neighboring objects to plants are; another plant, another tree, a fence, the grass, direction of air, and sun direction, that is if it is an outdoor plant.

If it is an indoor plant, the objects will be different, but still you want to maximize the use of the surrounding energies in a beneficial way.

If we consider a plant in a pot, first hold the pendulum and get the resonance or frequency of the pendulum adjusted to gold color, then hold the pendulum above the plant and with the other hand start rotating the pot, until the pendulum rotates clockwise, and here you stop as this is the best orientation for the plant. If you move the pot to another location repeat the same process again. See figure 7.

Figure 7

Once you have the plant in the best orientation you will notice a great improvement in growth and vividness of color.

In the case of a tree, usually a tree is placed in soil, use the pendulum the same way we did for the potted plant until it rotates clockwise, then place the tree or shrub in the soil, here you might need the help of someone else to hold the tree.

Here also you will notice the tree doing a lot better than the trees that were not oriented for maximum benefit of the environment

This way of orienting a plant or tree is very beneficial especially when you have an expensive species.

You can test the above procedures quite easily, for potted plants get two of them and orient one of them and leave the other at a random position, you will notice the difference within one week.

As part of my services of energy balancing homes and locations, I do the orientation for the plants as well, at the physical location, however it could also be performed over the phone, adjust the pendulum for gold color then ask the client to rotate the pot or tree, and once the pendulum rotates clockwise, you advise the client to stop rotation, as this is the right orientation, I usually ask the client to continue rotation then to rotate the plant in the other direction, just to confirm or double checking that this is the best orientation for the plant.

When plants and trees are properly oriented for maximum benefit of their surroundings; their S.H.E. works perfectly to the better of the plant or tree.

The above is a very simple procedure with great benefits for the plant and or tree, and with greater benefit to the client, as we are all proud of our trees and plants when they do well, plus having a good healthy plant in our environment.

Plants and trees are affected by insects and animals they are exposed to, a great way to protect your plants and trees, is after you perform energy balance and fix any breaks you find in the energy field, and after proper orientation as we mentioned, you place a protective shield around the plants as we did for people, and make sure the shield only allows beneficial insects to those plants, as some insects are beneficial to plants in one way or more.

The same guidelines and principals are also applicable when planting a seed, especially if you grow your own flowers or vegetables, and in particular the creation of the protective shield around the seeds.

When buying nutrients, insecticides, and fertilizers to your plants and seeds or soil additives, it is a good practice to consult your pendulum for a yes or no answer, and as an example you can say: is this – here you name what you are buying – beneficial to this – here you specify, seed, or plant or tree or soil – and see which way the pendulum rotates, if the pendulum rotates clockwise, then this is a yes answer, if it rotates anticlockwise, then it is a no answer, initially you adjust the pendulum to the frequency of the object you are asking for. If you have succeeded in using your mind in doing energy balance, you can use your mind to get the answer, and you will see in your mind which way the pendulum rotates.

When using your mind to get answers, you can see with your mind which way the pendulum rotates, or an even simpler method is to see which direction the energy will take, for example when I ask a question that needs a yes or no answer, I have programmed my mind to show me the direction, either right or left, if the direction is to the right, I consider that a yes answer, and if the direction is to the

left, then this is a no answer, this method will help you a great
deal in all your questions that need a yes or no answer.

Chapter 9

Color Balance

Colors are like what we see in the rainbow ROYGBIV, the letters stand for; red, orange, yellow, green, blue, indigo and violet.

Each color has its frequency, wave length and beneficial value, and a lot more that will be discovered in the future.

Colors are not there just for enjoyment, they are necessary for our health, and we need a balanced dose of colors every day of our lives, whenever there is a deficiency or an over dose of one color, a symptom starts developing, the purpose of the symptom is to tell us something is missing or something is wrong.

Color is vital for our S.H.E. performance. How do we know that we are missing one or more colors in our daily life, we use the pendulum and figure 8.

Figure 8

Deficient	Normal	Over dose
-	Red	+
-	Orange	+
-	Yellow	+
-	Green	+
-	Blue	+
-	Indigo	+
-	Violet	+

There are three readings for each color, deficient, normal and overdose, deficient in the figure is a minus sign - , and over dose is a plus sign + in the figure, the normal is the desired goal.

We hold the pendulum and adjust it to the frequency of the person we are checking the color balance for, then hold the pointer above each color's states, in sequence, once you do that you will notice the pendulum rotating clockwise at the reading of the color, if for example the red is deficient then at the minus sign for the red color the pendulum will go clockwise and back and forth for the normal and plus sign of the same color, then force the pendulum to rotate clockwise while the pointer is on normal red.

Repeat the same for every color as mentioned in the example above.

You can also use your mind to get answers as we outlined at the end of chapter 8, or even a simpler method just visualize figure 8, and as you ask the questions, see which area of figure 8 will be indicated, then also using your mind visualize the pendulum rotating clockwise over the normal column for the color in question. I do the following which is a lot faster and convenient; I first get to the alpha state, then ask the question "which color needs to be balanced", and I immediately get an answer by either showing me the letters of the color or actually seeing the color in my mind, you can do the same procedure, or devise your own way to get answers. Some people start doing the methods I do, then they either continue doing what I do, or come up with a different method for themselves.

If you are doing the color balance for someone else just add their name at the end of the above question.

Once I get an answer of which color needs to be balanced, I visualize the pendulum rotating in a clockwise direction over the normal for that particular color.

A point to consider, is that a person could be at the initial stages of being deficient or over dose for a certain color and symptom didn't occur yet, performing the color balance, restores the harmony of colors needed by the body.

Having a balanced color dose of all colors helps the S.H.E perform its duties normally for the well being of the person.

To know more about color and its uses, a good book is How to Heal with Color by Ted Andrews.

You can also do a search on the Internet for color therapy.

Chapter 10

Relaxology

Relaxology is the knowledge of relaxation.

The word Relaxology is not an English word and is not in the dictionary; however it infers the knowledge of relaxation that is why I use it, and I hope everyone would be knowledgeable on how to relax.

Relaxation is a much needed process for every person, if I may use an example here, like an elastic band, if you have it stretched all the time, it will reach a state where it will be cut, however if you stretch the band and then release it, this allows the band to avoid the state of being cut.

Relaxation is similar, if a person is continuously being stressed; a stage will be reached where that person has to give in and have an irreversible damage like when the elastic band gets cut.

Relaxation is very important for continuity of good life and good health.

The level of relaxation is also important, an ideal state is total relaxation, we are born good natured and we are born already relaxed, it is external factors that shape our present and future actions.

External factors are numerous, some of which are what we hear, what we see, all that touches our senses, those through the conscious or the ultra-conscious in a negative way, the most obvious is what we see on television, we see murders, obscenity, immoral behavior, subliminal messages that make us buy what we don't need, so many manipulative studies, and the list needs volumes just to list them and their effects on us and society.

Again relaxation is the key to being in good state of mind, and good state of health, practice it daily, even several times a day until it is a second nature, this way you control your destiny.

The TEENS concept is the best relaxation method available today, practice it yourself, and practice it with others and see the results for yourself. Teach people the concept specially your family. It is explained in the Hypnosis chapter.

As mentioned you can do the TEENS concept for yourself, and also you can do it for others, to relax them and remove anxiety, specially for closer people, if you already know what touches their senses in a pleasing manner, for example if you know your wife loves roses, just talk about roses and paint a very vivid picture of roses, you will find that your wife will relax immediately, and before discussing major issues use the same technique to ensure the discussion is objective and brings good results.

In the corporate world, the interviewer tries to relax the person being interviewed, so he can learn more about them.

Relaxation involves easy flow of thoughts, and a very good way when applying the TEENS concept as in chapter 12, is to never resist a thought that comes to mind, just let it flow by, if you resist the thought and start telling yourself that you are trying to relax, the relaxation process is interrupted, always remember that point of just letting the thoughts flow by.

Ideally you would like to be able to relax at will, and this what you will learn Hypnosis chapter.

Chapter 11

Exorcism

Everything is made up of cells and cells have positive and negative charges, leading to the formation of an electromagnetic field or energy field.

When people die, they are still made up of cells, they turn to dust and their energy field remains in tact and they have their own frequency, the dead have their world which is somewhere that no one knows where it is, I cannot claim to know where or how, the only logical knowledge is that they have their own frequency.

Some times those frequencies instead of going to their world, they go astray and for some unknown reason they attach themselves to humans, there are many speculative reasons, however they are not conclusive, causing a lot of strange behavior.

We all know what is normal, and we all know what is good, as this is the way we are created, however external pollution, external influences affect us, so whenever you see not normal behavior, and bad actions, it is due to some type of influence, in the majority of cases it is a bad frequency of a departed person.

Example of such people that have attached frequencies are, alcoholics, drug addicts, murderers, criminals in general, as it doesn't make sense for someone to do something wrong, in most cases those people have no idea or any clue as to why they are like that, nor do they know why they are doing what they are doing, they are destructive to themselves and others.

Most of these cases could be treated with exorcism and they will revert to being good people.

With Energy Balance, exorcism could be done to help those afflicted. The pendulum could be used to identify those attached frequencies, or it can be done using the mind, depends on which method you are comfortable with.

Whenever anyone has an attached frequency, their S.H.E. is with no doubt affected and performs poorly.

How does those frequencies attach themselves to humans, first they are energy fields that got lost and don't want to leave this world, and they look for opportunities of weakness within people, as for strong people they cannot deal with them. Strength is internal strength not muscular strength.

Once that frequency attaches itself to the human, strange immoral behavior is evident, with a net result of being destructive to oneself and others.

Those people don't listen to advice, they are there for destruction, in the majority of cases they destroy themselves, and those who love them are very much devastated.

To clear a person from that attached frequency, all you have to do is first identify that there is an attached frequency, using the pendulum or your mind, then commanding it to go to its world and never come back, and then mentally place a protective shield around the person we are helping.

Then check again as there might be more than one frequency attached, and then perform energy balance check to identify breaks and fix them.

It is quite a simple process and nothing scary about exorcism as you have been lead to believe, The important point is to get the permission of their guardian, specially if they are adults, as one always needs permission to perform exorcism and energy balancing.

One case I had, the client called me and told me his daughter is in bad condition and drinks a lot and stays out late, and hangs with the wrong crowd every night, so I asked for permission and after I received the permission I checked the girl and identified the attached frequency and gave the command to the frequency to go away and never come back, and using my mind I built a protective shield around her. The next day the father called me to thank me for the work done, and reported that his daughter stopped drinking and stays at home and smiles. I was very pleased that I was able to help.

Chapter 12

Hypnosis

Hypnosis is a great addition to the alternative medicine field; it is very useful in many conditions, like pain management, quitting unwanted habits, nail biting, bed wetting, self confidence, phobias, and in particular relaxation as we mentioned in chapter 10, plus a lot more situations could be helped through hypnosis.

Initially I was introduced to hypnosis through reading books, two books are in the recommended reading chapter 45. Then I realized that hypnosis would be a great addition to energy balance in helping others.

I attended a course run by Shelley Stockwell, who by the way is a great lady that will expose you to all what you need to know regarding hypnosis, where you will also practice hypnotizing others, and you will be hypnotized as part of the learning process. I learned a lot by attending the course and I am a certified hypnotist.

Once I knew more about hypnosis, I arrived at the conclusion that it is pure relaxation, of mind and muscles, more so the mind than muscles, as once the mind is relaxed the muscles will be relaxed as well.

After practicing hypnosis for a few months, I realized that some clients were apprehensive or afraid to be hypnotized, despite their belief that it will help them, and because I had a rule of never to force or trick anyone to being hypnotized, I wanted to arrive at a method that would remove any fears from being hypnotized, after having that desire and request to arrive at that method, I just let go and continued doing what I was doing. Several days later I arrived at the concept of no sleep hypnosis.

I have developed the Concept of No Sleep Hypnosis, for the benefit of the clients, as some were afraid to give in themselves for a hypnosis practitioner they met for the first time, the no sleep hypnosis allows the client to stay awake and still receive all the benefits of hypnosis.

Hypnosis is pure ultimate relaxation of all muscles, and once a person is relaxed they revert to their good self and can see all the solutions to their problems. We mentioned earlier that we are born naturally good, and when totally relaxed the pollution effects are non existent.

I also use energy balance before the hypnosis session, to clear any breaks, this way the hypnosis is more effective and brings the desired results faster for the client.

Total relaxation and No Sleep Hypnosis are achieved through the TEENS concept that I have developed.

The TEENS concept for relaxing at will and No Sleep Hypnosis is very simple to implement and even simpler to teach to people who want to relax at will, it is very important to relax as we mentioned earlier, and even more important to relax at will, you become in control of your well being.

The TEENS concept relies on relaxing each sense individually then all collectively.

T stands for Tongue for the sense of taste, and you ask the client what is the best taste you can possibly imagine, visualize it and keep it in mind. You can also ask the client to place that image in a specific spot, like at the left of the head for example.

E stands for Eyes for the sense of vision, and you ask the client what is the most beautiful thing they have ever seen, could it be the sunset, could it be a loved one, whatever is most beautiful to them, visualize it and keep it in mind as well, and place it to the right of the previous object.

E stands for Ears for the sense of hearing, you ask the client what is the best sound they enjoy listening to more than anything else, could it be the voice of a loved one, could it be the sound of the ocean waves, could it be classic music, visualize it and keep it in mind, and place it to the right of the preceding object.

N stands for Nose for the sense of smell, and you ask the client what is the best odor they have ever smelled, could it be roses, jasmine or a certain perfume or anything that the client feels is the best smell, visualize it and keep it in mind, and place it to the right of the previous object.

S stands for Skin for the sense of touch, and you ask the client what is it that when they touch they are out of this world, could be the touch of a loved one, or the touch of a certain texture, visualize it and keep it in mind, and place it to the right of the previous object.

Once you have made the client visualize an object for each sense, and placed them on the top of the head lined up from left to right, then you ask the client to collectively have them all visualized.

While you are working on each individual sense allow 5 minutes between each sense, so the client has enough time to visualize and feel that beautiful sensation and relax.

The last stage of collectively visualizing all the 5 objects in mind at the same time, here you allow the client as much time as they want, ten, twenty or thirty minutes.

Then you start asking questions about the problem and ask the client what they think is the best solution, and you can guide the client in thinking about the right answer, as sometimes they are so relaxed they don't want to get out of it.

Do the above TEENS concept for yourself and you will be amazed as to how you will be relaxed, and if you have trouble sleeping, you will sleep like you have never slept before.

You can help people who have trouble sleeping with the TEENS concept, with no pills, pure clean and safe way to get rid of sleepless nights.

Now you have learned the technique for no sleep hypnosis, and relaxation at will, which in my opinion is a very powerful method for helping people, and in most cases if you tell the client it is alright to close your eyes and sleep they will very happily, if they haven't already. The point to remember here is that sleeping or being hypnotized is the choice of the client, we have not forced anything or any method upon them.

The TEENS concept is very effective for people who have a test the next day, this way they get to sleep well and sleep the number of hours their body needs, and wake up relaxed the next morning, and use it before answering the test questions.

Another very valuable effect, is the client now knows what triggers relaxation, for example, whenever something upsets them, tell them to bring forward any of those 5 images to mind and the anger is gone, hence avoiding stress

Each individual should have those 5 images ready to bring forward, as this also helps the performance of the S.H.E., they can use an index card to record their choices for the senses, see as below, and replace the words visualized object with the chosen object for that sense, see figure 9.

Figure 9

T	Tongue for taste	Visualized object
E	Eyes for seeing	Visualized object
E	Ears for hearing	Visualized object
N	Nose for smell	Visualized object
S	Skin for touch	Visualized object

For children, they should sleep on a happy note (everyone should sleep on a happy note), and you can tell them every night to think of something they like best, and here this method serves several purposes, the most important is sleeping on a relaxed happy note which in itself stops nightmares, and they will wake up quite fresh and ready for a beautiful day. You can help the children by doing the same with them, telling them that you also will visualize hugging them.

The more often you do this with your child, the more they will be in control of their emotions, and they get to know how to make themselves happy, and after a while it will be an automatic process, leading to a happier life. Because the S.H.E. will have no thought pollution and will function smoothly to the better of the individual.

Chapter 13

Line Body Parts Balance

The human body is made up of trillion of cells all working perfectly getting their guidance and instructions from the master chip or master cell, with one objective, of keeping you in top condition.

So every part, every organ and in fact every cell are all interconnected.

To make matters comfortable to handle, the body parts and organs each will be represented by a line.

The line has no specific direction, as far as start and end, it is irrelevant where it starts and ends, remember all is interconnected.

You choose the part that represents the ailing part in the body, and then adjust the pendulum to the person's frequency, and hold the pointer over the line, start moving the pointer along the line to check if there are any breaks in the electromagnetic field or energy, there could be more than one break in each line. Once the break is identified by the pendulum going anticlockwise, force the pendulum to rotate clockwise and project gold into the break, and then place the pointer away from the line, then bring the pointer back over the line and see which direction it rotates, if it rotates clockwise, then the break is restored, if it rotates anticlockwise, then you need to force the pendulum to rotate clockwise for 30 seconds or more, again, and then repeat placing the pointer away then back on the line to see if the break in the electromagnetic field has been restored or not.

The following are the various parts of the body and you can draw your own lines, or use the lines provided here, you can start by using those lines, and then as you master energy balance, you can draw your own lines.

Initially, use the pendulum to identify which organ or organs have breaks, then work on each individual organ.

Hair,

figure 10

Forehead,

figure 11

Top of the head,

figure 12

Eyebrows,

right   left

left and right, figure 13

Eyes, left and right,

right   left

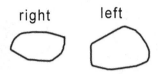

figure 14

Eyelashes, left and right,

right   left

figure 15

Nose,

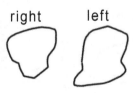

figure 16

Cheeks, left and right,

right   left

figure 17

Ears, left and right,

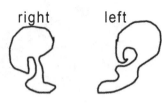

figure 18

Mouth and lips,

figure 19

Tongue,

figure 20

Gums, upper and lower,

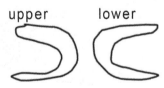

figure 21

Teeth, upper and lower,

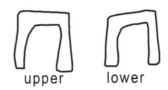

upper   lower

figure 22

Throat,

figure 23

Neck,

figure 24

Shoulders, left and right,

right   left

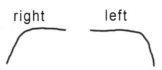

figure 25

Armpits, left and right,

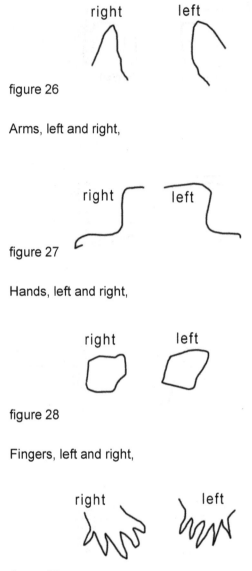

figure 26

Arms, left and right,

figure 27

Hands, left and right,

figure 28

Fingers, left and right,

figure 29

Chest,

figure 30

Breasts, left and right,

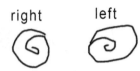

figure 31

Stomach,

figure 32

Small intestine,

figure33

Large intestine,

figure 34

Rectum,

figure 35

Scrotum,

figure 36

Gall bladder,

figure37

Pancreas,

figure 38

Liver,

figure 39

Kidney, left and right,

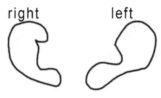

right   left

figure 40

Heart,

figure 41

Thigh, left and right,

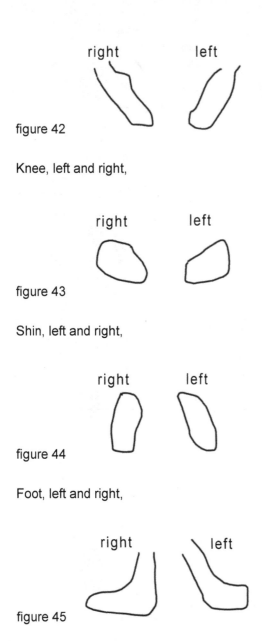

right   left

figure 42

Knee, left and right,

right   left

figure 43

Shin, left and right,

right   left

figure 44

Foot, left and right,

right   left

figure 45

Heel, left and right,

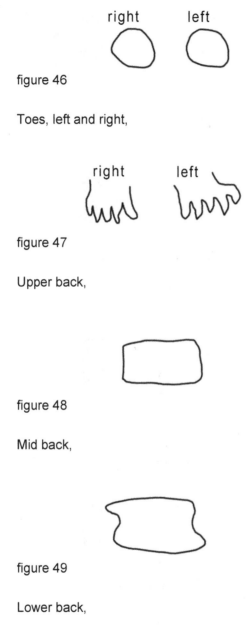

right   left

figure 46

Toes, left and right,

right   left

figure 47

Upper back,

figure 48

Mid back,

figure 49

Lower back,

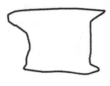

figure 50

Genital organs, male,

figure 51

Genital organs, female,

figure 52

You can of course use your mind as in energy balance advanced, to detect the breaks along the lines and restore any imbalance that exists.

Chapter 14

Visualization

Visualization is the creation of mental images; you already know about visualization, we have used it in TEENS concept to bring the happy causing objects forward.

Visualization works very well with energy balance and helps the results to last a longer period, and gives more power to the individual.

The best way to illustrate visualization is by example; several examples will follow.

When I used to teach in high schools, students for some reason are fascinated by crumbling a piece of paper and throwing it in the garbage bin, maybe they think it upsets the teacher, however with me, I told them to finish their work and then I will show them how to do that professionally, they were intrigued and finished their work immediately.

I told them to create a video in their mind of themselves throwing the crumbled piece of paper in the garbage bin, and it gets in every time, and instructed them not to think, just replay the video in their mind before they make the throw, those who played the video in their mind were able to do it even from a farther distance, and even one of the girls who never did throw papers in the garbage bin before, managed to get it in after playing the video in her mind, the majority of the class were extremely happy that they learned something new, I asked them to practice that over the weekend at home. The following week, I told them they can use that same technique of creating a video and replaying it in their mind to do anything they want, like answering all tests correctly, use it in sports, or music, and that it will make their life a lot simpler.

The idea behind the power of visualization is that the mind is more capable than you can ever imagine, and anything that touches our senses is recorded in our mind, then it becomes a matter of retrieving the information, when you consciously ask for information to be accessible when in need, the mind will do just that.

Another example that is tremendously beneficial, for a larger group of people. You are at work and you have a problem that requires a solution, all you have to do is visualize yourself finding the best solution, you continue doing what you normally do in similar situations plus adding the visualization, you will definitely find the solution a lot faster, and it will be a better solution.

Another example that pertains to work, is when you want a promotion, you want a certain position, or you want a raise, just visualize yourself being promoted, visualize yourself getting the raise, your mind and ultra-conscious will make you do the right things for management to grant you your wish.

Another example is playing golf for the first time, first watch a few games first then create your video and then go and play, you will definitely perform better than if you hadn't used the video in your mind, this is very useful if you have children and want them to excel in a certain sport, just let them watch those instructional videos of the sport or watch professional games, once they are born, of course the initial period should be 5 minutes daily for 3 to 4 months, then increase the time as they grow older.

The mind is more capable of enlisting the help of all the needed muscles to perform the desired action, you as an individual consciously have little knowledge of which muscles are needed, however your mind knows which muscles are needed and how to use them as well in a coordinated manner.

For some people, replaying the video once could be sufficient to perform the action, for others it might take replaying the video several times, or even several days.

For those who have children, it is wise to show them how to visualize as early as possible, as this will increase their self confidence and esteem, because they will be more capable than those who don't visualize.

One time when my son was in grade seven, he had a test to see how he remembers the 50 states and their capitals and the proper spelling, I told him take a snap shot of the map and keep it in his mind, and he did that, and after the test I asked him, what did he do in the test, his reply was he did very well and that he used the image he had stored in his mind to remember some of the states and the spelling.

You can practice visualization for your work and relationships, to achieve the results you desire.

Warning; once you create a video, don't, I repeat, don't doubt your abilities.

Using visualization with energy balance adds quite a lot of power to the S.H.E., for example after knowing where the break is in the electromagnetic field, fix the break with energy balance, and at the same time visualize yourself free of pain and free of discomfort, and you are in perfect condition, this way you also closed the door on thought pollution.

Some people have a habit of saying the wrong thing at the wrong time, all they have to do is visualize themselves saying the right thing at the right time, and replay that scenario in their minds many times, it only takes a few seconds to replay the scenario, so it can be done a hundred times a day quite easily.

Another example, you want to be a better driver, visualize yourself being the best driver there is, you want to play sports better, use the same method.

As mentioned earlier, the number of times an individual needs to replay the video or scenario depends on the person and the results they want to achieve.

Doing the visualization techniques on many aspects of your life, will help you reach the stage of visualizing automatically without even thinking about the issue, as by then your mind is well trained to do what is needed.

With visualization you achieve

Better performance

Enhanced S.H.E. activity

Getting rid of thought pollution

Chapter 15

Power of the mind

The mind is very powerful, beyond anyone's imagination; the mind stores all types of information in a greater capacity than any existing computer, processes a lot more information than the most capable computer and faster as well.

To use our mind effectively, first we must acknowledge the fact that our minds are powerful and that there are no known limitations, so all you have to do is explore and test what your mind is capable of, for example light up a candle and place it 2 feet away from you and see if you can bend the flame to the right or to the left or forward or backward using your mind.

A valuable tool like our mind must be protected from all pollution, which comes in various forms, as we discussed earlier, like thought pollution.

If you value your mind, then it makes sense to protect your whole body, as it is one system that communicates and interacts for your well being, it doesn't make sense to keep your hands clean and then eat junk, sure your hands are clean, but your stomach has taken food that will be distributed to the rest of your body.

The point is that any pollution whatever it is, and no matter how small it is, will affect you one way or another with the ultimate effect on your S.H.E. performance.

How do we know if what we are eating is junk or not, read the ingredients and don't eat food with artificial colors, artificial flavors, and man made chemicals.

You can use your pendulum to know if a certain food is good for you or not, don't rely on studies, as most studies have another objective in mind, you should be able to read a study and only get out of it what is good for you, use your pendulum to know the validity of the study for you, or use the mind as we described earlier.

Using the pendulum and getting answers, is a powerful method, that will guide you to what is beneficial for you, the more you use the pendulum the more your ultra-conscious knows that you want what is right, and eventually you will find yourself doing what is best for you, as the message is in the master cell now.

How do we tap into those great powers of our minds?

If you have reached that point in the book, you are on the right track; I mean reading is one of the great ways to get information, read as much as you can, as all the information is stored for later processing when in need.

When a book or a piece of information is placed in front of you or comes across as a friend's recommendation, or just reading it leisurely, this happens for a reason, there is nothing called by chance or by accident, it is only that we don't know why, and we have an urge, or we have been programmed to have a reason that we can relate to for everything, of course there is a reason for everything, but we don't usually know it, it is all part of the universal master plan.

Of course eating the right food goes without saying.

It is quite important to have the desire to know what you are capable of, as long as you have the desire to know, you will recognize the unique powers that you have once they are presented to you.

Now you know you have a powerful mind and you are set to tap into its powers and you want to know what those powers are, having that thought is good enough to start the process of revealing those powers to you.

You might find out that you are psychic, you have extended vision where you can see beyond the normal vision, you might discover that you are able to communicate with animals, the list is endless.

Because I have the above thought in my mind at all times, I discovered many things I can do, like communicating with the departed people, being able to do remote viewing, I can read aura colors, I can raise the temperature by two degrees Fahrenheit of a thermometer, I can mentally know directions with my eyes closed.

I believe every individual has something unique and special; it is just a matter of finding out what it is and when, some discover it early in life, some later in life, and since we don't know how long we will live for, early or later don't really mean much.

Always have the above thought in mind and you will discover wonders.

The power of the mind, is limitless, your mind will do what you want, for example if you want to be healthy, just say "I am healthy", always use the present tense and also see yourself healthy, this enables the mind to work on that and keep you healthy and keep all pollution away from you.

If you want to be rich, just say "I am rich and have plenty of money and I am happy", your mind will immediately work to fulfill what you desire.

However be careful what you say or think, because if it is a wrong thought, your mind will do it for you as well.

A very important condition in tapping the power of the mind is, once you say or think what you want you must let go and forget about it and go on with your life as you normally do, because if you don't chances are it will not be done, because, let me explain it using an example; if you say I am healthy, here the mind starts to fulfill that for you, however if you think about it again you might start telling yourself, well I am not a super man, may be I get the flu once a year, if something contagious comes across, I will get infected, do you see what you did here, you put the wrong thought to your mind that will start working on fulfilling it for you.

That is the main reason people don't get what they want, they doubted themselves and started adding wrong unwanted thoughts, and unfortunately this happens automatically without you realizing what you are doing, important to catch yourself doing that and stop doing it.

The master chip and S.H.E. work very well for your benefit until you place those wrong thoughts, so use your mind power for your well being.

There are many books on mind power, however all you need is the desire, and you will have it.

Chapter 16

Listenology

Listenology is the art of listening with the intention of helping, I am an expert listener and all people I listen to, that have problems, their problems are solved, and most of those solutions come from them.

Listenology is not an English word, but it presents the closest meaning to what I do, so I am a listenologist practicing Listenology.

The best solution of any problem is only existent and found within the person who has the problem.

The solution of any problem for an individual involves known variables and unknown variables at the conscious level.

The known variables are already known, like I know I need money, I need to talk to a certain person, I need to give in, I need to do this or that. That is the easy part of the variables and if used alone to find a solution, the solution will become a problem and will need a solution in a short while.

The most important variables are the unknown variables, I mean by unknown being unaware of. The master chip knows what is best for us, even if we consciously don't know; the master chip stores information since our inception till now, all our parents' teachings, all our religious teachings, everything we have been exposed to is stored in the master chip, whether it came through the commonly conscious 5 senses or through the ultra conscious

All that information has made us whom we are and made us reach where we are and most definitely has the solution to the problem.

The reason that some people are known for finding solutions, is not that they are smarter, they just have a wealth of information and a lot less thought pollution, they eliminated the words difficult and problems from their vocabulary.

I believe everyone has the same level of smartness; it just shows differently in different subjects and shows differently in different aspects of life, some people are good in mathematics, so those in the mathematics class think they are smart, others are very good in English language so those in the English class would say they are smart, in simple terms nobody is dumb, and could be called otherwise in the mathematics class. We all have the same level; it just shows differently depending on the knowledge and what we want.

If we have the solution why doesn't it come out to mind as we need it, and it would be a great problem free world.

The only reason, the solution is not obvious is the CIRCLES and that the mind follows the path of least work.

Circles are loops of certain behaviors we are engaged in, some call it routines; let us examine a family of a husband and wife and a son and a daughter and two grandfathers and two grandmothers.

Look at figure 53 and note the following:

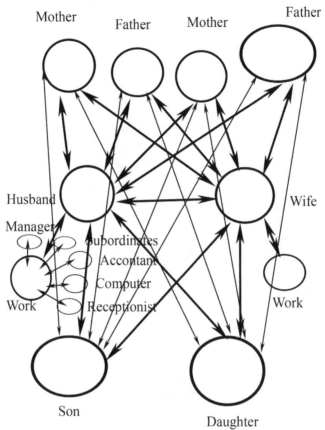

53

Keep in mind that the loops are a type of automatic behavior we engage in, in relation to the subject we are interacting with.

The husband deals with son the same way in every issue, with the daughter also has a set way of dealing with her in various issues, the same applies to his father, his mother, his wife, his rest time, his sleeping way, his wake-up routine, his work, his house, his father in law, his mother in law, his friends, his tools.

The home has its loops as well, the garage, the back yard, the plumbing, the wiring, the telephones, the kitchen, the lights, the TV, the stereo.

The wife has the following loops, her husband, her son, daughter, father, mother, kitchen, house, mother in law, father in law, work, car, back yard, garage, and bedroom.

You will notice that the son and daughter show up in both husband and wife loops and they are both different loops, as well also in the grandparent's circles.

The work for example has its loops, and sub loops like subordinates, managers, accountant, computer, and receptionist.

Look at the diagram and you will see many loops that you can extend to many more loops.

The point is we have enough loops on our hands that we have no time to think outside those loops or circles.

The mind follows the path of least work, ideally no work at all, the mind will do what it is set to do every time in the same situation.

By listening and asking questions and making the person look at those circles and loops from the outside, the solution will come to mind, and those are the best solutions because they are from the person himself.

To make people arrive at the best solution to their problem, all you have to do is create circles and loops for them, then make them step outside and have a second look, and you can try that for yourself, just draw your own circles and loops and look at them from the outside, use figure 54 or make your own.

Figure

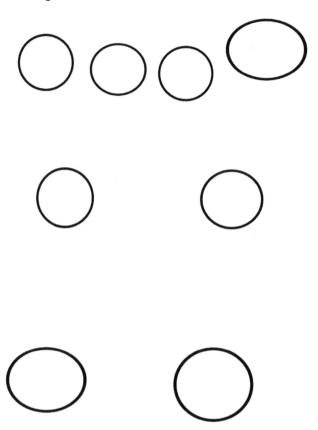

One has also to remember that each individual sure has the same conscious senses, however reactions are different, and the ultra conscious senses and their reactions are also different. Each individual has their own logic, if you go further, most people have the same objectives, like a good life, good health, good children, good house, good car, and a lot more; however what is good for someone could be the opposite for someone else, for example, a small car could be acceptable for some and totally unacceptable for others, it all depends on one's logic.

Keeping the above point in mind when you discuss issues with friends or relatives or coworkers or children will make you understand why they are different and why they aren't difficult with you, they just have a different logic. Mastering this understanding will make you a good listener and a good problem solver.

Chapter 17

Psychic Surgery

Psychic surgery is a process where you mentally go inside the person's body and with energy balance you get to know where the break is in the energy field, and go to that area and see what is wrong and fix it by projecting gold to the break, and while you are inside the body, you will find yourself moving to where the help is needed, the first time was an amazing experience for me, and the results were immediate relief for the client, in some cases you have to do the same process more than once, specially in cancer cases.

Another aspect of psychic surgery is that while you are inside, you can make any devices that will do a certain task, like for example if someone has high cholesterol, leave a device in their body that cleans the blood stream from the excess cholesterol, to reach a balanced state of cholesterol, usually one would leave the device running for seven days.

The design of the device is left up to you, design it based on what you know with the objective and intention of performing a certain task, to increase the effectiveness of the device always project gold onto the device.

When to use psychic surgery, this is up to you, as with the other methods in the book here, you will find many techniques and methods, you will find some will work in certain situations and some will not work in other situations, choose whichever you are comfortable with, and as you use the different methods you will find yourself being drawn to one method automatically without even thinking about it.

Psychic surgery is quite useful in cases where the symptoms keep reoccurring, symptoms reoccur for a reason, and until you find the cause of the symptoms, this method is of great help.

This is my version of psychic surgery, you might find it being explained differently in other books, and may be you would have your own method for psychic surgery, it is all names, what counts is your self confidence and what you believe you can do.

How I do psychic surgery is very easy, read the next section.

I visualize a glass container to be placed in front of the person and this device is connected with plastic tubes to both arms of the individual, I visualize that body fluids are coming out of the right arm into the glass container for clearing all whatever is the cause of the ailment, and at the same time project a gold color swirling clockwise around the container, for a period specified as needed, then after the treatment of the fluids in the container they go in the body again through the left arm, and this is left for seven days running automatically, taking fluids from the right arm, going into the container treated with gold all around, then back through the left arm. For added benefit, mentally project gold color to the arms where the tubes are connected.

I had a client in Germany who asked for help, so I mentally installed this device and to my amazement, the container got shattered to pieces, because of the amount of metal that was in the body fluids, so I installed a more robust container and left the device running for seven days. The next day I contacted the client who confirmed that he was using a silver compound to do a type of flush, and I knew then why the first container got shattered. A week later the client reported great improvement and feeling a lot better and disappearance of symptoms.

Chapter 18

Cancer

Cancer is when the cells don't communicate well together and just become very active more than normal and create havoc and total disruption of functions that could lead to killing the person.

Cancer in reality is that cells are not communicating, communication lines are closed for some reason, with energy balance you can detect where the break is in the electromagnetic field and fix it, or you can use psychic surgery to install a device that will restore communication between cells, once communication is back to normal, cancer is gone, there has been many cancer cases that has been helped by one method or another.

I have worked on cancer afflicted people and for most of them the symptoms disappeared and they are still alive with no cancer issues.

I will illustrate what happens with cancer patients by this case.

There is this lady who had an appendix operation, and during the surgery they found two orange size tumors, the appendix and tumors were removed and the tumors analyzed.

The report on the tumor indicated that there is something not normal that they called cancerous.

The lady contacted me for help, and I did energy balance and detected where the breaks were and fixed them, and in my opinion, what was diagnosed is gone and no longer there.

However the doctors wouldn't believe me and ran all possible tests to try to locate the cancer, and all their tests proved there is nothing wrong, but they still hang on to the first tumor report, and thinking that they can not be wrong, reached a decision that the cancer is in the ovaries and since the lady is over seventy, they concluded that the body doesn't need those parts and might as well remove them, strange thinking.

My comment on the body doesn't need them, it is a totally wrong statement that displays arrogance, if they are right why didn't the creator who made a trillion cells work in harmony made the unneeded organs dissolve, who is right, I am sure you can figure it out.

Anyway they operated on the lady and removed the ovaries and had them analyzed and also found nothing wrong and everything is normal.

Still hanging on to the first tumor report, thinking again they cannot be wrong, and despite the fact that they were wrong in removing the ovaries, they still recommended chemo therapy.

This time the lady told them enough is enough and just stay away from me, and to this day after 2 years she is living as healthy as ever.

During the stage of trying to convince her with chemotherapy, they quoted numbers that chemotherapy helps and eliminates a percentage of the risk, and makes you in a better state statistically. My comment on that, even if chemo reduces the chance of being sick by whatever percentage, it really means nothing, because for an individual, you have no ideas to which group you belong, and it is either that group or the other, so it is a 50% chance both ways, forgetting that 100% of chemo therapy recipients get side effects that are quite devastating.

My comments here will be a little bit strong and hopefully eye opening.

The present system dictates certain procedures that must be adhered to by practitioners, for if they don't they could be sued or could lose their license, and we don't want them to be in jeopardy, so the responsibility is yours, you are the one who should make the decisions, not numbers dictating what you should do.

You might meet some clients that are convinced by the numbers that chemo therapy is acceptable, here you can do energy balance to lessen the effects of chemo therapy, and I have done that for a very close friend of mine who never smoked, but had lung cancer, he took the treatments, however the side effects of the treatments were so minimal because of the energy balance methods performed.

Chapter 19

Autism and Syndromes

Autism is a disease or a condition that afflicts kids. One time I attended a lecture about autism and I was surprised to know that its rate in 2004 is 1 in 250 children being born, ten years ago the rate was 1 in 1000, and only 10% of those 1 in 250 are within families that had autism before, so 90% are new cases, the traditional field have no idea how this can happen, and the lecture was presented by a physician who has an autistic child.

My opinion on the matter is that the people who are giving birth today could have been consuming junk food and drinks most of their lives, plus medications, plus they could have been exposed to the invisible pollutions, not even mentioning the invisible pollution during pregnancy, it could be one or more of the above reasons

No doubt the ova and sperm have been affected, and when combined the result could be autism or other diseases. If the parents continue their life style or continue being exposed to the invisible pollutions, the pregnancy period adds up to the final outcome.

As said earlier, research is a business, so why would anyone research what I am saying, it has no profitability, and if I am right, there will be so many law suits all over the world.

As a result of the above the S.H.E. is impaired and that could be the cause of autism.

Here we can still do energy balance as I have done in the example mentioned earlier in chapter 6.

Syndromes are many types, and what is mentioned for autism would also apply to syndromes.

A good internet group for parents with autistic children is

http://groups.msn.com/AUTISMCHATANDSHARE

Chapter 20

Allergies

Allergies are a reaction within the body to something sensed by any of our five senses, in fact not only the conscious five senses, but also the senses of the ultra conscious also detect imbalances of a different nature and react to them causing allergies, this latter type is not even considered in the traditional field and may be that is why it is hard for them to cure allergies, or even know where they are coming from.

There are so many theories; I say theories because they are not conclusive.

There are allergies to food, smell, sound, touch, and vision.

Cause of allergy could be internal within our bodies or psychological like in case of sound and vision, these are sometimes called phobias. Although the psychological factor could be so strong that it is hard to identify as psychological.

Sound and vision allergies are easily handled using hypnosis, energy balance.

Here the trigger in most cases is an earlier experience that caused severe pain, and the reaction that is initiated is for protection from a repeat of this pain. Once the cause is found out and neutralized, the person is no longer allergic to those sound and vision triggers.

With energy balance you identify the place in the mind where this information is stored and make the pendulum rotate clockwise hence disassociating the pain with that experience, quite a simple technique that benefits many people.

The other allergy types of taste, smell and touch could be helped with energy balance, use the pendulum and the anatomy book to locate the break in the electromagnetic field and rotate the pendulum clockwise while projecting gold color, or do the same with your mind.

Using the mind or the pendulum and anatomy book is really a matter of choice and you should use the method that you are most comfortable with. In some cases you will find yourself knowing the answer and where the breaks are before the pendulum moves, and in other instances you will use the pendulum.

The important point is that you use the method that brings you the most desired results.

Energy Balance techniques are very simple to perform, if a traditional practitioner was to write about allergies, they probably would write a 100 books, but as I said with energy balance methods are a lot simpler, and right to the point, and brings faster results than any known method.

Chapter 21

Headaches and Migraine Headaches

Headaches and migraine headaches are very common among a lot of people, and there is no cure especially for migraine headaches, there are many medications that hide the symptoms.

From personal experience I get headaches when I haven't eaten, and when I didn't have enough sleep, to me the headache is a signal that I need to eat or need to sleep.

Once I eat or sleep the headache is gone, many times the solution is right there, we need to observe and analyze just a touch more the symptoms and possible causes in our actions and in our environment.

I was lucky to discover the cause of my headaches, however many people are not as lucky, and when I do energy balance to get rid of headaches for people, the headaches go away, however they return if what caused them in the first place is still within the environment or is affected by the invisible pollution.

Headaches could be caused by many factors, anywhere in the body so you need to use the pendulum and an anatomy book to find the cause, or use your mind, once the break is found make the pendulum go clockwise while projecting gold color and that should clear the cause of the headache, and the headache goes away, this energy balance method is a lot faster than any pill found today.

How long does the energy balance effect lasts for, I will answer that question with an example. If one was to burn their finger from the stove for example, it will heal after a few days with a new layer of skin, however if we get burnt again from the stove, we will suffer again. Usually the symptoms returns if the cause is not identified and made neutral.

In addition to using energy balance, one must identify the cause, especially if the symptom keeps recurring. I had a client who kept contacting me for a bladder area pain, I perform the energy balance and the pain goes away, however within a few hours the pain comes back, I perform energy balance again and the pain goes away, but later the pain comes back, for a full two weeks the pain kept coming back, until I started asking questions, as to what the client does regularly, and I discovered that it was mineral water that the client drinks a lot of, by the way the majority of mineral water types have a lot of salts and extended use of mineral water will increase the amount of salts in the body and the excessive use of mineral water becomes a type of pollution.

I advised the client to stop the mineral water and to the benefit of the client the bladder pain never came back.

Chapter 22

Arthritis

Arthritis so far has no cure in the traditional field, despite the technology and knowledge available, that only means one thing, their knowledge is limited, and there are a lot more diseases that have no cure in the medical field, plus many other diseases are of unknown origin.

There is nothing wrong with having limited knowledge, it is admitting to the fact that makes the difference, so many medications claim to cure arthritis as seen on TV, when you see those commercials, you think the medication will take you to heaven, and by the way that is the intended effect for the gullible.

Industries and corporations thrive on the present state of Arthritis; to them an arthritis patient is a client for life.

Arthritis is easily treated with energy balance, I remember a client complaining about foot pain, so I asked for permission, and once granted I located where the break is in the electromagnetic field and sent energy to that area, and the client said, "I feel as if someone lubricated my foot, feels very good, as I have gout.", gout is type of arthritis.

I had another client in Australia, who couldn't walk because of severe arthritis in the feet, I asked for permission and once granted, I located where the break is in the electromagnetic field which was in the heals and shin, and used my mind to fix the break, and the client was able to walk comfortably again.

For treating with energy balance using the pendulum and anatomy books or the mind, it makes no difference what the disease is, the system is the same regardless of the disease name, however it is good for making the client grant you permission without reservations.

Chapter 23

Anti-Aging

Aging is a natural process that all livings go through at a certain time in their lives, however in recent times aging has accelerated, diseases and symptoms are occurring at earlier ages.

Symptoms of aging are numerous; the most obvious ones are wrinkles that happen due to weakened muscles and the skin losing its elasticity.

It is not important to list the symptoms, the important issue is to realize that it will happen, and will happen faster and at an earlier age if we don't eat well, don't sleep well, and don't take care of ourselves.

There they are the initial cure for delaying aging, eat well, sleep well and take care of yourself.

Doing the above will definitely make your S.H.E. perform its functions as intended, for your well being.

With today's technology and genetic engineering and the abundance of dead food, so many ingredients that are needed by the body are no longer there, or are available with a much smaller quantity, for example to get the value of a carrot that used to be eaten 20 or 30 years ago, you have to eat at least one pound for every carrot, however that is too demanding, but if you use that pound to make carrot juice and drink it, then you are close in value to what used to be in a carrot 20 or 30 years ago.

The same goes for many vegetables and fruits, if you can make juice, by all means do, and it is a lot healthier than any supplements you would buy.

With energy balance and your mind you can do a great job to slow aging.

Do energy balance and clear all the breaks in the electromagnetic field, and immediately after, condition your mind that you are doing and eating what is beneficial to you, very simple process, once you set your mind, what will happen is that if you come across a food you know is junk your mind will not make you eat it, and at the same time you will not feel deprived of something you like, as we have to admit that junk food tastes great, and that is one sense if you control well, you are on your way to a healthier life.

There are many methods on the market; however I believe what I just explained above is quite sufficient to get you the results you want.

Energy Balance is the simplest form of healing and the most effective as well, and produces the fastest results.

For aging issues I use DNA methods, however I couldn't explain it or talk about it better than the author Vianna, check her books as mentioned in Recommended Reading chapter 44. Very simple methods are explained by Vianna that bring good results.

Chapter 24

Back Pain

Back pain is very common to people from all walks of life, be it upper, middle or lower back pain.

To handle back pain using energy balance, either use your mind to locate the break in the electromagnetic field and fix it, or use the pendulum and the anatomy books.

The location of the pain is not necessarily the same location for the break in the energy field, sometimes a toe pain originates in the back. I am mentioning this so you are aware of this fact.

Many times you locate the break and ask the client or the person you are doing energy balance work on is this where you have pain, you might get a no, and that will affect your credibility, it is always better to ask the client about where they feel pain and then you do your work in locating where the break is and after getting permission, fix the break. Usually you don't need permission to locate where the break is, however you must have permission before performing the energy balance.

Back pain is unfortunately so common, and I have helped so many people, more than I can remember with back pain.

However one case I remember, the client had middle back pain and pain in the back of the head, I managed to locate the break and restored the balance to the energy field for the breaks causing the back pain, however not for the pain of the head, despite that I was given permission, the energy wouldn't go through for the head pain, I relayed that information to the client and told him sure you have given me permission but it was for the back, and not for the head as you were afraid, he confirmed what I said, and my comment to him was, whenever you feel comfortable to give permission for the head, to let me know.

I quoted this example, to show that sometimes permission is only for one break not all the breaks, so you know why the energy doesn't go through sometimes.

Chapter 25

Misleading Numbers

Facts need to be stated first before getting into the misleading numbers.

Research is a business; think about a multi billion dollar corporation that spends a hundred million dollar on research, do you think for one second they would welcome research results that are not favorable to them, no way of course, it is a business, and if a researcher dares to report an unfavorable research, they get penalized by never getting any research funds, and chances are they will not get employed by research companies or universities, as those companies employ researchers that bring them more research funds.

This point of view was mentioned in a less severe tone in in many other publications.

This point is proven case after case, by the medications that have been withdrawn off the market, someone is at fault here, and if it has been researched honestly and properly it wouldn't have been in the market in the first place.

Another fact is that those who have set the safe guidelines are the same ones that provide the money, maybe not directly and could be through a third or tenth party.

To know who is behind a certain research, just trace it to who will profit from it, and use your judgment.

Another fact is people have been made to accept research and to never question it.

So if you have enough money and a product, you can easily make a good return on investment, just get a research done.

It is said for example that a certain disease costs ten billion dollars; here we have to question who is actually paying and who is making a good size fortune.

Regarding who is paying, everyone pays

Who is making the good size profit, of course the entity that the research was made for.

Also we should ask, out of these ten billion dollars, how much or what percentage is an income to someone or an income to a corporation that employs many people, so the truth is, even if it is spent, it has created jobs and put food on the table for many families. What is the real net cost, if any at all.

I am sure those numbers are there, but they are never publicized.

You can apply the above way of analysis to all those big numbers and realize the truth for yourself.

Chapter 26

Dead food and live food

Food can be classified as dead food or as live food.

Live food makes the S.H.E. perform its functions, while dead food deprives the S.H.E. of its needed resources to function optimally.

Dead food is what has very minimal nutritional value if any at all, and is made of chemicals and additives.

Live food is the true organic food, I say **true** organic because there is some food that is classified as organic but is not.

Technology and profitability has controlled what we buy to eat, many vegetables and fruits are picked and taken away from their natural environment before ripening and placed in coolers, and then artificially ripened with gases before being sold, this is an unnatural way to ripen foods, and definitely has an effect on our system and our S.H.E., although it is said to be safe, because it doesn't cause directly diseases, however that missing ingredient sure has an effect.

Wax is applied to fruits and vegetables, to stop them from going bad, you must wash them in a way to get rid of the wax, I do that by using vinegar, or don't eat the outer waxed layer. Another point is are we sure that wax didn't permeate through the skin to the inside of the fruit or vegetable, even at very low levels it is still not healthy. Also this is classified as safe.

What a safe world we live in today.

Genetic engineering to fruits and vegetables, the fruits and vegetables got bigger and lost taste, it is the older generation that remembers how it used to taste, the newer generation that is all they know.

So if genetic engineering has altered the taste, something must have happened, maybe it lost one of its ingredients that were there for us to benefit from. The unfortunate part is that seeds are genetically engineered, so it might be organic, but already tampered with.

Where can you get the un-tampered with seeds, probably from a third world country, and then you face customs that tells you, you cannot get those seeds in, they are worried about the agriculture of the country, but always remember that who ever puts the rules in place, have a vested interest.

When we ingest tampered with food we are affecting our S.H.E. functions, and then we wonder why we are sick and why we get cancer. Maybe one of the reasons they can not find a cure for cancer is that they continuously tamper with food so variables keep changing, and also that is why there are so many new diseases, and diseases have been observed to occur at a younger age than they used to.

Beef and cattle, originally cows eat grass naturally growing in pastures, however because of limited science knowledge they started making ready mixes of food to replace grass, the result is beef that is not as healthy, and so as the milk that comes out of those cows. The same is done with chicken and hence the chicken and eggs are not as healthy to us as they used to be.

The best method to detect what is beneficial for you from what is not is to use the pendulum.

If you reach the stage of using your mind instead of the pendulum, you have an advantage, because you can detect things quicker and no one will look at you when you use the pendulum in the supermarket. Your health is more important than people looking at you, think about it.

Because of genetic engineering and pesticides, food has been altered and many needed ingredients are missing and the vitamins and minerals market has boomed to reach a few billion dollars in sales annually.

The supplements market also is quite enormous for the same reasons.

You hear about a newly discovered food ingredient in a certain country, and all tests show a positive result to justify selling the product.

This is a fallacy because this type of food with that ingredient is there for a reason, it is beneficial for people who live there, they have their environment and other factors that necessitate its presence, every country or locale has its own fruits and vegetables for one simple reason, it is for that habitat and for those who live there.

Of course you can eat those imported foods or take those researched supplements, but they are not as beneficial as they are claimed to be.

The ideal food is the naturally grown food and the food that is grown in its season.

To have a balanced food intake, consider the rainbow colors, ROYGBIV, red, orange, yellow, green, blue, indigo and violet, make sure that every day you eat food that has all colors, ideally every meal should have all colors.

Follow those guidelines when selecting foods and your S.H.E. will function a lot better.

How to eat to help your S.H.E.

Use natural candy and this what you tell kids that it is natural candy, and they will love it as they have been conditioned to take candy, if you say natural, kids will not understand, and once a child is of the age to eat everything, make sure you give them a lot of natural candy like lettuce, tomatoes, fruits and so on.

The required discovered vitamins are:

A – B1 – B2 – B3 – B6 – B12 – C – D – E – K

The required discovered minerals are:

Calcium – Phosphorous – Magnesium –
Sodium – Potassium – Sulfur – Iron – Iodine – Zinc – Copper
– and others

To know if one is deficient or over dosed for the above vitamins and minerals use the pendulum with figure 55, and 56, applying the same method explained in chapter 9 Color Balance.

Figure 55

	A	B1	B2	B3	B6	B12	C	D	E	K
Deficient	-	-	-	-	-	-	-	-	-	-
Normal	A	B1	B2	B3	B6	B12	C	D	E	K
Over dose	+	+	+	+	+	+	+	+	+	+

Figure 56

	Calcium	Phosphorous	Magnesium	Sodium	Potassium	Sulfur	Iron	Iodine	Zinc	Copper
Deficient	-	-	-	-	-	-	-	-	-	-
Normal	Calcium	Phosphorous	Magnesium	Sodium	Potassium	Sulfur	Iron	Iodine	Zinc	Copper
Over dose	+	+	+	+	+	+	+	+	+	+

I use the word discovered, because that is what is known at this time, and there is a high probability that more could be discovered.

The ideal way to ensure you are having all the needed vitamins and minerals is to eat a variety of fruits, vegetables, and fish and meat, there is no magic pill, however having a good mix of foods will ensure you have all what is needed.

The easiest way to know that you are eating a variety of food is to go by colors of food, it is a lot easier than trying to know what vitamins or minerals are in each type of food, for example lettuce is green, tomatoes are red, and carrots are orange, and so on.

Chapter 27

Success Formula

The first thing to do to succeed is to get rid of pollutions mentioned earlier.

Pollution will hold you back, and will affect your S.H.E. so you will not get to your real potential.

Why do people succeed in one thing and not the other, because they treat different matters in a different way. Every person on this earth has succeeded in some type of activity or thought, at least once, like when you first walked, you definitely at the time had no thought pollution and was determined.

I am sure you can find a success story within your life, recall that success and check the following reasons for the success you had, it could be one or more of the following:

1. You loved what you were doing

2. You had more information than others

3. You have no pollution, specially when you are still a child

4. You treated it as a challenge

5. You had no other choice

6. You wanted it so strong that you visualized it unknowingly

7. Other reasons ....

Once you have identified your success and how it came about, if you do a repeat of the same process in any other issue you will succeed the same way you did before, remember it is you the same person that did it before.

This is the number one formula for success.

Your earlier success whether you know it or not, has involved a good performing S.H.E. with no pollution, involved visualization, and involved listenology, and self hypnosis. Read those chapters again and you will realize that you used all those tools unknowingly and that is why you succeeded.

Having a good performing S.H.E. with no pollution, especially thought pollution makes you ahead in your success plan.

You knew exactly what you wanted and you knew what needs to be done, so it was automatic visualization.

You listened either now or earlier, in fact you must have listened at both times.

You relaxed to be able to function better; you realized the value of rest and relaxation.

You must have also done a lot more than what I noted above, think about it and do use what have worked before to succeed in the new endeavor.

So now that you know what it takes to succeed, your success should be reached faster and a lot easier in any endeavor you set your mind on.

Chapter 28

Remote Viewing

Remote viewing is when you are able to see what is there without physically being there, some call it astral travel. I have read about astral travel, and that scared me enough not to try it, as they say there is always the possibility you cannot get back to your body. However remote viewing you stay where you are and get a vision of what is there as if you are just in that place.

Remote viewing is very helpful in analyzing conditions at homes and work places to identify causes of pollution, especially the invisible pollution.

When I perform remote viewing I am able to see things, many times while I am talking to friends over the phone or over the internet, after taking permission I am able to describe what is in the room or home.

One time I was asked by a client to check their apartment for undesirable objects that are present. I started with the living room and there I found an empty metal box on top of a book shelf, I asked the client to put it away, actually the client had this box there and forgot about it, metal objects have a lot of magnetic frequency that could interfere with the S.H.E..

Then I viewed the bedroom where I found a cupboard, I asked the client to open the right door and look at the second shelf from the top, there is something there that is causing pollution, the client responded there are clothes there, I said under the clothes there is something black and heavy, the client then reached under the clothes and got out a device that is used to remove the tags attached to clothes as you see in stores.

This is one example of remote viewing; the most important thing is to get permission to do remote viewing, other wise it is like stealing.

You can perform remote viewing just the way I did, you relax and breathe deeply and start the remote viewing session.

Relax using the TEENS concept as in chapter 12.

Breathe in a deep relaxed manner

Start remote viewing to what you have permission to view.

Initially you do the relaxation, and deep breathing consciously, and when you do that, you are at a level of brain and mind function that allows you to do all what I mention here, after performing this several times, you will find that it takes you less time to be at that brain and mind state to do all energy work you want to do.

One point to always remember, is that don't force the issue, if you don't get to succeed in remote viewing the first time, it is not the right time, and immediately stop thought pollution and start again, don't give up just stay with it and to help the issue visualize that your remote viewing is bringing a lot of happiness to many people and you are doing it successfully.

To help you in remote viewing you can start practicing at home and remotely view what is going on in another room in your house, or any other place you want to remotely view.

Chapter 29

When did things happen?

All through our lives things happen, our lives start at inception to today, what happens could be called accidents, I say could be called accidents, because there is nothing called accidents.

Things happen for a reason, and the ignorance of the reason makes people call it accidents, it is a lot easier to call it an accident rather than trying to find a reason, so many people have had accidents where they felt so bad, like those getting to the airport to catch a plane that they missed because of an accident on the way, later to discover this plane crashed, then no one is happier than them, they got to know the reason for the accident which in this case, was to make them miss the plane.

Many times we don't recognize the wisdom behind things that happen, it is not necessary to know the wisdom, however it is important to recognize that there is a wisdom system that operates for our benefit.

Many times things happen that upset us, or make us think it is the end of the world, and to our surprise what happens was a blessing in disguise, like what happened with me and my foot pain, with that sequence of events I got to know and learn about energy balance from Vince Kaye, that foot pain was a door opener to so many good things, most of which I am able to help people.

Using the pendulum and charts provided you can tell exactly when things occurred.

You can even get to know the date and time.

For fun you can find the date and time when certain things happened, you can easily surprise your friends, and have a lot of fun doing it.

However for the purpose of doing energy balance and helping people we want to know the things that happened that caused a break in the electromagnetic field, and which effect is still present and affecting the person and for sure affecting the S.H.E..

Having that knowledge helps in locating the root cause of many symptoms, and once you have identified the date, do energy balance and fix the break at that time period, and the results are astounding.

Here is how it works:

You first want to know how many things that happened, that still have an unfixed break in the electromagnetic field or energy field.

Use the number chart, see figure 57, from 0 to 9; use the pendulum to get the first digit and then use the chart of Yes and No, see figure 58, asking the question: is there any more digits, if No then this is the number of things that happened, if Yes then use the 0 to 9 chart to identify the second number, then the Yes and NO chart and so on until you have identified the number of issues that took place that still has an unfixed break in the electromagnetic field or energy field.

Figure 57

0   1   2   3   4   5   6   7   8   9

Figure 58

YES   NO

If the number of happenings is 9, you write them as follows:

1

2

3

4

5

6

7

8

9

You get the frequency of the 1st happening and then use the year, month and day chart, see figure 59. You will notice that the year part is just 4 rows of numbers from 0 to 9, the first row is for the first digit of the year from the left, the second row for the second number to the right of the first digit, the third row is for the third number of the year to the right of the second number, the fourth row is for the fourth number of the year to the right of the third number. The year could possibly be 0963, meaning it happened to an ancestor and has been passed on through the generations. If the year number is greater than the present year then it is BC (Before Christ) if you are determining the year and now is 2005 and you get 2010 for example that means it is 2010 BC, and whatever happened to an ancestor has passed on through the ages, through some system.

Figure 59

Year	1st	0	1	2	3	4	5	6	7	8	9	
	2nd	0	1	2	3	4	5	6	7	8	9	
	3rd	0	1	2	3	4	5	6	7	8	9	
	4th	0	1	2	3	4	5	6	7	8	9	
Month	1	2	3	4	5	6	7	8	9	10	11	12
Day	1	2	3	4	5	6	7	8	9	10	11	12
	13	14	15	16	17	18	19	20	21	22	23	24
	25	26	27	28	29	30	31					

You first identify the year using the year part of the chart see figure 59, by holding the pointer over the first row and see above which number it will go clockwise, then the second row, third row, and the fourth row, once you find out the year, write it next to the 1 above, then you use the months chart to identify the month by asking which month the 1st incident happened, here also hold the pointer over the months part of the chart, and see which month the pendulum will go clockwise for, and write it down next to the year number and then use the days chart asking which day of the month did the 1st incident happened to identify the day, see also where the pendulum will go clockwise, and write it next to the month.

Now you have identified the date of the 1st incident, to get to know the hour of the day this happened use the time chart, see figure 60, asking which hour of the day the 1st incidence happened, and note which hour of the day the pendulum goes clockwise, to identify the time of this occurrence, write it next to the date for the 1st incident.

Figure 60

1	2	3	4	5	6
7	8	9	10	11	12
13	14	15	16	17	18
19	20	21	22	23	24

Now use the body chart, see figure 6, to know where the break in the electromagnetic field is and rotate the pendulum clockwise.

Here you can go as deep as you want into the body using the anatomy book; the decision is up to you.

Do the same for the other incidences and write them down accordingly and fix each break in the electromagnetic field as you get to them.

Of course you remember that after you have adjusted the pendulum for the 1st incident, you use that frequency for all that is related to that 1st incident and you keep the pointer on the chart, and don't forget to adjust the pendulum according to the number of event you are working on.

After performing the above procedure several times, you can use your mind to get the answers instead of the pendulum and charts, this is a faster way; however either way is fine, it is a personal preference, use which ever way you are comfortable with. Using the mind will allow you to see the exact numbers for the year, month, day and hour as well, definitely a lot easier and faster as well.

The purpose of initially using the charts and the pendulum is to provide you with some guide as to what to look into, as later you can have the chart in mind and immediately identify the dates just as easy.

Fixing all those root breaks for the person you are doing this for, will definitely make them feel so great they will thank you so much, you will be amazed yourself at your accomplishments.

The value of this is that you have helped restore the functionality of the S.H.E., which has been afflicted with some breaks for many years, and you would have stopped the inheritance chain.

Chapter 30

Protection

In all facets of life we need protection, to ensure our S.H.E. is working and doing its functions properly to our benefit, from various sources as outlined below

From ourselves

This is the internal thought pollution – ITP - we mentioned earlier.

From others

This is the external thought pollution – ETP – we mentioned earlier.

From Insects

Let us say you live in a home where on a monthly basis you hire someone or a pest control company to spray your home to get rid of ants and insects in general.

Regardless what anyone says and regardless what any study says, chemicals sprayed are harmful, and should be avoided as much as possible.

Energy balance is a lot safer and cleaner, and keeps the S.H.E in good working order.

First you do energy balance for the place and fix any energy breaks, then you flood the place with gold color, and while you are doing that you are telling yourself "I want the place free of all types of insects".

To flood the place with gold, you can either do that mentally by visualizing a shower of gold covering the whole place, or use the pendulum and a sketch of the place, and adjust it to the gold frequency and rotate the pendulum clockwise until you know that the whole place is gold, you can always test what you have done either with your mind or with the pendulum, have the pendulum on gold frequency then go around the place and check if the pendulum moves clockwise or not, if it does, then you have completed the work, otherwise repeat the earlier steps of flooding the place with gold.

Some of the benefits of moving away insects from your place that way are:

No chemicals to inhale

No chemicals stuck to the walls and floors

You have not killed the insects

Usually this method lasts for two weeks, then you have to repeat it again, and that is from personal experience.

From harmful thoughts and Invisible Pollution.

Some people are in the habit of talking about others in their absence this is a common occurrence, it is unfortunate but it happens, no one should talk about someone else badly, either praise or just keep quiet.

Create a shield around you, similar to an egg shell and fill it with the gold color and have the desired effect in mind, for example, any harmful energies coming my way to be returned to source with love.

The size of the shield is up to you, you can make it with a distance of two feet in all directions from you, or ten feet, you assess and decide what is the best distance.

Another example of thought when you are creating the shield, I always want a distance of two feet between me and a specific person or animal. I used that technique whenever I visit my brother who has a German Shepherd dog who loves to lick people, and I don't like to be licked by dogs, so I created the shield with a five feet distance, and if I walk toward the dog, the dog goes the other way and stops at the five feet distance I have set for my shield.

This is an example of the power of energy balance, and you can have other needs for creating your own shields.

Chapter 31

Memory

The memory is where information is stored for later processing and retrieval, either automatic or on demand.

Many times for no apparent reason we remember something, it is not apparent for the conscious mind, but definitely is known to the ultra conscious mind, or better to say for the master chip.

That memory was brought to our attention for a reason, to serve a purpose to our benefit. Examples are many, like remembering unconsciously a happy memory, this happens either to make us in a good frame of mind for what is to come, or to get us out of bad mood we might be in.

By the same token, if we are not balanced and due to external frequencies, a bad memory might unconsciously be retrieved, to annoy us, to make us do things leading to undesirable effects. We have to remember that being in an unbalanced state and a less than good state of mind opens the door to external frequencies to get attached to us.

Usually a lower state of mind is self inflicted, meaning; we opened the door or allowed the door to be open to such frequencies.

We should always be ready with the five images we created using the TEENS concept as in chapter 12, and have them come to memory immediately to protect our state of mind.

It is expected for every person to be in a down state of mind due to multitude of reasons; biological or psychological, at one time or another; however the difference between a person and another is how long it takes you to overcome that down state.

With the five images from the TEENS concept you can overcome the down state very quickly and at the same time preserving your good health, as when we are down certain chemicals are released in the body, and when we are on the upside state another set of favorable chemicals are released in the body, this latter set of chemicals are the beneficial type for the body.

The more we consciously use those images; a state will be reached where it becomes automatic retrieval of those images within split seconds in the time of need; here the master chip knows what you want to accomplish and will do it for you faster than you consciously can, read this again and be aware of this fact.

The above statement provides great value to preserve the function of the S.H.E., at all times.

Chapter 32

How to communicate with the Master Chip

The master chip runs every function in our system, at the conscious level and at the ultra conscious level.

The master chip is the highest control system within our body, it probably has many names, however the names don't signify any specific value, the important thing is that there is a master chip that governs every cell within our body.

The ultra conscious and conscious are the main communication channels to the master chip.

Each of the conscious and ultra conscious has their duties; the ultra conscious runs all of the body functions under the supervision of the master chip, whether we are awake or asleep the body functions keep on working in perfect order. The conscious mind controls our conscious commands, like raising our hand, moving our legs to walk, we decide to walk consciously and it is done, unless the ultra conscious decides otherwise for our benefit.

Commands and wishes are passed to the master chip through the ultra conscious and conscious.

It is quite important to realize that the ultra conscious has its language, some say it doesn't understand the negative statements including no, not, a famous example; if I tell you do not think of a pink elephant, you will say that consciously, however you immediately think of a pink elephant, why, because the ultra conscious didn't understand not in do not think. You have to be careful how you say things or you are giving the wrong undesired commands to the ultra conscious and that is what you get.

The S.H.E. is greatly affected by what messages the master chip receives through the ultra conscious and conscious. Then it makes great sense to observe what we say, what we listen to, and all what we are exposed to.

An ideal way to know once and for all how you communicate to your master chip is to be aware how many times you say no and not and in what context, whether you say it out loud or within yourself it has the same effect on the master chip.

Once you are aware of how you communicate, you will get an insight as to why you might get sick and why things are not happening as you wish.

It is a simple exercise, with great benefits; the goal is to send the right messages and commands to the master chip.

You can also visualize that all you do and all you think is be for your well being and your benefit.

Chapter 33

Responsibility

We have a responsibility toward ourselves and towards everything else.

We have to keep our S.H.E. in good environment by eliminating all types of pollutions discussed earlier, we should watch what we eat, we have to be aware how we talk and think to prevent the wrong messages going to our master chip.

Our objective is to live in good health and in good surroundings, and this can only be achieved by keeping all the wrong things out.

Use the TEENS concept to relax and once you are relaxed you will know what is right and what is wrong for you, use also the pendulum to confirm your findings.

If you have a family, it is your responsibility to teach them how to preserve their S.H.E. as well.

Responsibility towards everything else other than us is a huge responsibility, however easy to deal with.

When we look at something or think about someone or something, we project energy to whom or whatever we thought about or looked at, so if your thoughts are negative, that is the type of energy you projected and your projected negative energy is pollution to that object, plus it might return to source. It is your responsibility to fix what you have projected, if you had good thoughts, you projected good energy, for a second imagine if every person on earth did just that and projected good energy what the world would be like, it would be heaven on earth. That is the size of your responsibility.

Another very common example is when you see someone who is down, you either talk to them or think to yourself, he or she looks terrible, you just projected negative energy and affected their S.H.E., what you did was create external pollution to that person, and it is your responsibility to fix what you did, by either helping the person or at least send them a good thought which is good energy projection.

Another common example, is when you see a tree that is not fortunate to look pretty in your eyes, so you say either to a friend or to yourself, that tree looks terrible, you again projected negative energy that affects the S.H.E. of the tree, and it is your responsibility to fix what you projected, by projecting a good thought, by either saying or thinking "May the tree gets better".

Also it is your responsibility when you see someone else projecting negative energy, either to educate them, or to send a good thought to nullify the earlier sent negative energy.

Warning: Projection of this undesirable energy is quite dangerous to some extent, as sometimes it is returned to you; I had this happen to me four times, until I realized this truth.

One time I was walking down the street and saw someone walking in a different way, so I said within myself, why doesn't he walk properly it is funny, the next day I developed a condition where I had to walk the same way, and had to have surgery. Six months later without realizing; I did the same thing with another person walking in a different way as well which I ridiculed in myself, immediately the following day I was walking the same way and had to have surgery again.

The third time I saw someone who couldn't bend his knees properly, so I ridiculed him within myself, same thing happened to me the next day; I couldn't bend my knees properly for 4 years after that. Finally I got the message that when I send such thoughts I get them back, so I stopped making fun of situations like that, and whenever I see someone doing things differently I pray for them, and wish them well.

Despite my above realization and me being careful, I did it one more time and when I saw this lady having a different looking finger, I ridiculed her in myself, a split second wrong thought projection, caused the same symptom to me the next day as well.

I said to myself after this last incident, I need to protect myself from myself, and said everything in this world is good regardless how I think, and I will project good energy when needed to do that, I drilled this statement in my mind by keeping it in mind all the time until it became automatic. I learned my lesson the hard way; I mentioned those examples to spare you similar occurrences.

Now you know your responsibility and what you really can do; either good or bad, the decision is yours.

Wrong energy projection can come back to source, and good energy projection can also come back but with good energy to build our reserve of good energy for the welfare of our S.H.E..

Chapter 34

A Day's Anatomy

Let us have a look at a day, what do we do, we project energy to ourselves and to everything else around us, it could be good energy or bad energy, before reading this book, you could have unintentionally projected good or bad energy, with the possibility that it was returned to you, and caused discomfort if it was the wrong type of energy.

Now you know what bad energy is and what good energy is, all energy projected comes back under reciprocation, so if you send good energy you get good energy back, you send bad energy you also get it back as well.

When you project good energy and get it back you are creating an ideal environment to your S.H.E., and you are building up your supply of good beneficial energy that will become of use when we are on a down cycle which is inevitable, remember we said earlier that a down cycle will happen and what matters is how long it lasts before you pull yourself out of it. The more the reserves you have the faster you are out of the down cycle.

When you project bad energy, you get it back and you are depleting your reserves and your S.H.E. will be affected adversely.

Our objective is to provide a good working environment for our S.H.E. and the master chip, by projecting good energy and as we said earlier it comes back, we also build our reserves.

Let us analyze a day of our life.

Starting by when we open our eyes in the morning.

What is the first thought that comes to mind and what type of energy is projected, observe what thoughts come to mind and what is the first thing you say, to start a day, you should project good energy as soon as you open your eyes in the morning, that is how a day is started right and on a good note.

Then you start getting ready for breakfast, what do you do then, what type of energy do you project, do you watch TV and get thought pollution, observe your actions.

Then you get dressed after a shower, and you are ready to leave the home to go to work for example, how do you leave the home, what good thought did you leave the home on, leave on a good thought that projects good energy so it would come back to you when you get back after work.

You then get into your car, what goes through your mind, is the weather good or bad, regardless what the weather condition is, always project good energy.

While you are driving, do you listen to the radio and get thought pollution or do you listen to classic music, and what goes through your mind as you see the other cars and the streets, be careful what you project here, as you get back what you project.

Then you arrive at work, and as soon as you come across the first person, what type of energy you project, good, bad or nothing, it is always good to project good energy and start the working day on a good note.

As you interact with your colleagues, regardless what happens, always project good energy that becomes your reserve that you are building for your S.H.E., and for the remainder of the day at work.

Then you are ready to leave, the same way you left your home projecting good energy, also leave work projecting good energy, as you will get it back the next day.

Wherever you go; always project good energy, and if a bad energy slips and is projected, fix the situation immediately.

As you are driving home, what goes through your mind, do you keep projecting bad energy to yourself, like I had a hard day, I am tired, this is thought pollution that depletes your reserves of good energy needed for your S.H.E. to function and protect you. No matter what the day at work was always project good thoughts and energy.

Now you are at home, if you have left good energy as you left in the morning you will get it now, so build on it and keep projecting good energy to all for the ultimate result of preserving your S.H.E.

You eat dinner and do certain things, whatever you do remember to project good energy.

Then you are ready to sleep, always make sure you project good energy before you sleep, as it will be there for you when you wake up in the morning.

Observe and project good energy for seven days, after the seven days, you will be projecting good energy automatically for ever, and that is what is needed for your S.H.E., it is a loop you are getting yourself into, however a very beneficial loop and way of life, which is quite simple to do.

Chapter 35

Invasion of the Master Chip

The master chip as we mentioned earlier is the top and highest control system of the human body.

Let me put it this way, if I want to manage you, and control what you do, for my benefit. The easiest and most effective way is to provide your master chip with the messages that serve my purposes; for example; the majority of people all over the world now believe research, we said earlier that research is a business.

How did people come to believe research, this was done in a very professional way to add credibility, most people believe those who have a higher degree, and those who wear a white coat, so initially all research only came from people with a doctorate degree and or also from those who wear white coats, after this was drilled in people's minds, any research is easily believed, so manipulation has become easier and controlling peoples' habits, especially purchasing habits couldn't be easier than that.

Look around you and go to a supermarket and or a drug store and see how many items have low carb on it, although this is just a marketing scheme and has nothing to do with real health value, however enough research was published on TV and Radio and print media to make low carb as the savior, then when another product is ready, research will come out to discredit low carb and claim the newer product is the new savior.

This is just one example, another example is the way kids are raised to believe whatever is on TV, so they become good consumers all their lives.

Another example is the medication advertisements; they make people think that if they want to be in heaven they must take that medication.

If you think for a moment, you will find this is done in all facets of life, eating, clothing, health issues, what to tell your children and what not to tell them and it has reached a stage where people will not do anything unless there is a research to justify the issue, forgetting or not knowing that research is a business.

I am only mentioning those invasions, so that you are aware of what is going on, and unfortunately all those invasions affect the S.H.E adversely, and you become a good consumer to pills.

Just be aware and protect your S.H.E. and your master chip by using common sense, and be aware of impulsive actions, just observe your actions and one of the ways to know if that specific research is good for you or not, is to use the pendulum.

The best method to protect yourself from invasions is to construct a shield around you that stops all types of invasions to your master chip.

Create the shield by relaxing then visualizing a protective layer like an egg shell around you and fill it with white or gold that will stop all invasions from getting to your master chip.

Chapter 36

Ball of Energy

This energy can be felt and then placed where the pain is with very good results.

Position your hands as if you are holding a ball with both your hands in front of you, keeping a distance of four to six inches between the palms of your hands. Move your hands away from each other and bring them close together in a slow motion way, you will start feeling the area between your hands filling up with energy.

Now you have created a ball of energy, then fill that ball with gold or white color, then you can place it where the pain is, for example, if the pain in the knee, place the ball in a way that the knee is inside the ball, and rotate the ball of energy clockwise around the knee, this method can be applied to many types of pain specially arthritis and headaches.

You can apply this method in two ways, the first we already described above when you have client with you. The other way is, after creating the ball of energy send it using your mind and visualization to where the person's pain is, here there are no time or distance limitations, for example; the person who needs your help called you over the telephone and asked for your help, first ask where the pain is, then ask for permission to send energy, then create the ball of energy, then use your mind to send it where it will do good, and rotate it clockwise.

You can apply the same method to animals, dogs and cats and birds and plants as well.

To add more power to the ball of energy, make it gold or white in color.

Chapter 37

Human Radar

The human radar system has been around for ages, a mother always feels her children, she might wake up before they need anything, or when something goes wrong it is usually felt by the mother, to a lesser degree fathers as well could have the human radar system, in fact everyone has it, it is matter of turning it on, by being aware that you have it.

Sometimes you could be faced with a situation where your help is needed, but there is no way of communication within a certain period, so in order to provide help as needed, you can become a human radar for that person for that time period. All you have to do is do energy balance for the person and fix all breaks in the electromagnetic field or energy field, then tell yourself from now till I communicate with the person or I stop the process I am to detect all requests for help by that person and name the person.

There is a story of how I got to know about using the human radar system, I am mentioning this example to demonstrate that once you are open to helping; many things can happen and you can discover a lot more things that you are capable of.

I had a very close friend who gets feet pain and he was going away for 3 days where there will be no possible communication, he asked for my help for those days in case pain occurs, my immediate response was, just let me know, then he reminded me that he will not be able to communicate for those three days with me, so I agreed to help and because I wanted to help so much the following occurred. During the second day I felt a foot pain similar to what my friend gets, so I did energy balance for him and my pain was gone. When he returned I asked him about the foot pain, and he confirmed it and also confirmed that it went away within minutes of getting it.

I don't do the human radar technique very often, only in cases of emergencies, and for my children and mother, as sometimes they don't want to tell me about their pain. But if the need arises it could be done quite as easily.

Possibilities of what you can do once you know energy balance are limitless, because you are dealing with things in a different way and in a different level altogether. You will definitely discover for yourself.

Chapter 38

Sleep, and how to make use of

Sleep is part of our life and an important part, we spend a quarter to one third of our lives asleep, some sleep six hours, some sleep eight hours.

The basic rule for waking up is that we should feel good and well rested anything other than that is not acceptable and will have its toll on our health and our S.H.E.

If we wake up not feeling good, then we have to stop and think as to why this happened, did we get to bed late, did we add any electrical equipment to the bedroom, like a television, a video an electric alarm, did we sleep with our wrist watch which is battery operated, were those gadgets close to us, did you sleep with the television on all night.

A very dangerous thing that many people do is going to sleep with the television on and hugging the remote control. How is that dangerous, the remote control has a battery which creates a magnetic field that interferes with our electromagnetic field, so does the television. Another danger is the content of the programs being played on the television, when we are asleep our conscious mind is asleep; however our master chip is running the show and is bombarded with all that is being played on television through the ultra conscious, which could be a type of pollution.

The best way to sleep is to sleep on a happy note, use the TEENS concept as in chapter 12 and have those images in mind using visualization, and make a habit of doing that every night as you go to sleep.

After sleeping on a happy note, now you have a chance to use those sleeping hours beneficially.

The subject here is sleep learning, you can learn whatever you want during your sleeping hours, for example you can have a CD or cassette player running all night with the subject of your choice, the volume could be low, as now it is the master chip and the ultra-conscious that is absorbing the information not your conscious sense of hearing. You can record using your voice whatever you would like to learn during your sleep, and have it playing during your sleeping hours, you can learn another language, you can listen to religious recitations, you can listen to selected stories to enhance your vocabulary and your literal ability, just think of what you can learn during your sleep, if you sleep six or eight hours every night that means that you have 2190 or 2920 hours during a year – 365 days – or 91.25 days or 121.66 days every year, see how much time you have that you can put to good use.

If you play appropriate material to your kids when they are asleep, you will be amazed at how fast they progress, and you can start doing that as soon as they are born.

Use your sleeping hours wisely and you would add 33% to 50% to your awake time, if you sleep 6 hours then your awake time is 18 hours, then the 6 hours of sleep is 33% of the awake time, if you sleep 8 hours then your awake time is 16 hours, making the 8 hours 50% of your awake time.

Quite a gain when you use your sleep hours wisely, so use it and enhance your S.H.E..

Chapter 39

Lab Test Numbers

There are so many laboratory tests, from blood to urine to whatever they can get their hands on to test.

Every test or as they say lab work has several readings, normal, and not normal, and normal for men is different from normal for women.

The value of lab tests is to know how the various interactions in our bodies are performing; usually what is called normal is a range, as what is normal for men is different from what is normal for women, what is normal for a child is different from what is normal for a person over sixty, and so on. They provide a guideline to the doctor.

So whenever your lab test results show a deviation from normal numbers, there is always a reason, however the first thing we need to establish, if it is normal for us to have this reading, here we use the pendulum, get the person's frequency then hold the pointer over the reading and ask is this normal for that person, the pendulum will either go clockwise or anticlockwise or sideways, clockwise means yes, anticlockwise means no, sideways means the question is not answerable the way it was phrased, if yes then you don't need to do anything, if no then rewrite the range you want to test, and use the pendulum again for yes or no, if sideways then rephrase the question.

You have to be aware that not normal readings from lab tests are an indication that something is wrong, which in turn will affect your S.H.E., here you use the pendulum and make it rotates clockwise for the normal reading to get rid of that situation and get back to normal, with good results for your S.H.E.

Some of the tests done are:

Acidity (pH)

Alcohol

Ammonia

Amylase

Ascorbic Acid

Bicarbonate

Bilirubin

Blood Volume

Calcium

Carbon Dioxide Pressure

Carbon Monoxide

CD4 Cell Count

Ceruloplasmin

Chloride

Complete Blood Cell Count (CBC)

Copper

Creatine Kinase (CK or CPK)

Creatine Kinase Isoenzymes

Creatinine

Electrolytes

Erythrocyte Sedimentation Rate (ESR or Sed-Rate)

Glucose

Hematocrit

Hemoglobin

Iron

Iron-binding Capacity

Lactate (lactic acid)

Lactic Dehydrogenase

Lead

Lipase

Zinc   B-Zn

Cholesterol

Triglycerides

Liver Function Tests

Magnesium

Mean Corpuscular Hemoglobin (MCH)

Mean Corpuscular Hemoglobin Concentration (MCHC)

Mean Corpuscular Volume (MCV)

Osmolality

Oxygen Pressure

Oxygen Saturation (arterial)

Phosphatase, Prostatic

Phosphatase

Phosphorus

Platelet Count

Potassium

Prostate-Specific Antigen (PSA)

Albumin

Globulin

Prothrombin (PTT)

Pyruvic Acid

Red Blood Cell Count (RBC)

Sodium

Thyroid-Stimulating Hormone (TSH)

Alanine (ALT)

Aspartate (AST)

Uric Acid

Vitamin A

White Blood Cell Count (WBC)

Once you know your normal range value for the test result, write on an index card the name of the test and the reading you want your lab test to show, see figure 61.

Figure 61

Cholesterol test   150 to 200

Then use your pendulum, adjust it to the person's frequency then hold the pointer above the reading you want as written on the index card, and force it to rotate clockwise while projecting gold to the desired reading. Then repeat the same process the next day, however first check which way the pendulum rotates, if clockwise, then this is the present reading if you were to have a lab test, if the pendulum was to rotate anticlockwise, then the required reading hasn't been achieved yet, and you repeat the above procedure again of rotating the pendulum clockwise.

How do you get the normal range value, either ask your doctor or check the internet for such values, and then consult your pendulum to see if this is the good value for you or not.

Chapter 40

Diseases and Specific Energy Balance Treatments, <u>Orothemes</u>

There are so many diseases; the medical profession has a name for everything that happens to us.

Here you will find energy balanced images for each disease listed here, as well as body parts and organs, including front and back, and the energy balanced image, Orotheme for each.

If you happen to be afflicted with any of those conditions listed here, just rub your hands together and place one hand over the image so you touch the image, and most important is to allow the energy to help you.

If a part of your body is aching or making you feel uncomfortable, choose the appropriate image for that area and rub your hands together and place the palm of your hand on the image, so you are touching it, and of course allow the energy to help you.

If new diseases are discovered, and you know which organ is affected, use the organ images and also rub your hands together and place one hand over the image, so you are touching it, and again allow the energy to help you.

How long should you rub your hands together, maybe 5 or 10 seconds.

Which hand should I use to place over the image, the hand that is most comfortable placing on the image, it makes no difference, and the most important part is allowing the energy to help you.

All the Orothemes are energy balanced, for the specific disease or area of the body or the specific organ mentioned.

Once you are able to do energy balance, you can also create images that would help people and energy balance those images the same way I did, I used my mind to energy balance all those images.

It is very important that as you place your palm on the image, to visualize a pyramid coming out of the image and going through the center of your palm into your body filling it with energy and gold color to combat that disease and restore normal functionality to the organ.

The value of Orothemes is that they are energy balanced to help those who have those conditions. Don't change what you are doing unless what you are doing is a type of pollution, then use the images to help you, and decrease the side effects of medications if you are taking any, and never stop medications without consulting your doctor.

For children, you can help them rub their hands together then place their palm on the image, the same also applies to those who cannot do that by themselves.

After those images, there is a list of images for body parts and organs that you can also use to restore your electromagnetic field or energy field.

Abdominal Injuries,

figure 62

Abscess,

figure 63

Achondroplasia,

figure 64

Acid-Base Imbalance,

Acidosis,

figure 65

Acne,

figure 66

Acoustic

Neuroma,

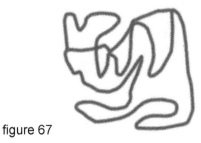

figure 67

Acromegaly/Gigantism,

figure 68

Actinomycosis,

figure 69

Acute febrile respiratory disease,

figure 70

Addison Disease,

figure 71

Adenoma,

figure 72

Adie Syndrome,

figure 73

Adiposis Dolorosa, Dercum Syndrome,

figure 74

Adrenal Gland Diseases,

figure 75

Adrenoleukodystrophy,

figure 76

Afibrinogenemia,

figure 77

African Sleeping Sickness,

figure 78

Agammaglobulinemia,

figure 79

Agnosia,

figure 80

Alagille Syndrome,

figure 81

Albinism,

figure 82

Alexander Disease,

figure 83

Alkalosis,

figure 84

Alkaptonuria,

figure 85

Allergy,

figure 86

Alopecia,

figure 87

Alpers' Disease,

figure 88

Alpha-1 Antitrypsin Deficiency,

figure 89

alpha-Mannosidosis,

figure 90

Alphavirus Infections,

figure 91

Alport's Syndrome,

figure 92

Alstrom Syndrome,

figure 93

Altitude Sickness,

figure 94

Alzheimer Disease,

figure 95

Amaurosis Fugax,

figure 96

Amblyopia, Lazy Eye,

figure 97

Amebiasis,

figure 98

Amino Acid Metabolism, Inborn Errors,

figure 99

Amnesia,

figure 100

Amniotic Band Syndrome,

figure 101

Amyloidosis,

figure 102

Amyotrophic Lateral Sclerosis, ALS,

figure 103

Anal Cancer,

figure 104

Anaphylaxis,

figure 105

Androgen-Insensitivity Syndrome,

figure 106

Anemia,

figure 107

Anemia, Hemolytic,

figure 108

Anemia, Iron-Deficiency,

figure 109

Anemia, Macrocytic,

figure 110

Anemia, Pernicious,

figure 111

Anemia, Sickle Cell,

figure 112

Anencephaly,

figure 113

Aneurysm,

figure 114

Angelman Syndrome,

figure 115

Angina,

figure 116

Angina Pectoris,

figure 117

Angioneurotic Edema,

figure 118

Anisakiasis,

figure 119

Anisocoria,

figure 120

Anomia,

figure 121

Anophthalmos,

figure 122

Anosmia,

figure 123

Anoxia,

figure 124

Anti-Glomerular Basement Membrane Disease,

figure 125

Antiphospholipid Syndrome,

figure 126

Antithrombin III Deficiency,

figure 127

Anxiety Disorders,

figure 128

Aortic Valve Stenosis,

figure 129

Apert Syndrome,

figure 130

Aphakia,

figure 131

Aphasia,

figure 132

Apnea,

figure 133

Appendicitis,

figure 134

Apraxia,

figure 135

Arachnoid Cysts,

figure 136

Arachnoiditis,

figure 137

Arnold Chiari Malformation,

figure 138

Arrhythmia,

figure 139

Arteriosclerosis,

figure 140

Arthritis,

figure 141

Arthrogryposis, Guerin-Stern Syndrome,

figure 142

Ascariasis,

figure 143

Asperger Syndrome,

figure 144

Aspergillosis,

figure 145

Asplenia,

figure 146

Asthma,

figure 147

Astigmatism,

figure 148

Astrocytoma,

figure 149

Ataxia Telangiectasia,

figure 150

Athlet's Foot,

figure 151

Atrial Fibrillation,

figure 152

Attention Deficit Disorder,

figure 153

Autistic Disorder,

figure 154

Ayerza's Syndrome,

figure 155

Babesiosis,

figure 156

Back Pain,

figure 157

Baker's Cyst,

figure 158

Balanitis,

figure 159

Baldness,

figure 160

Bannayan-Zonana Syndrome,

figure 161

Barre-Lieou Syndrome,

figure 162

Barrett Esophagus,

figure 163

Barth Syndrome,

figure 164

Basal Cell Nevus Syndrome,

figure 165

Batten Disease,

figure 166

Beau's Lines, Nail,

figure 167

Beckwith-Wiedemann Syndrome,

figure 168

Bedsore,

figure 169

Behcet Syndrome,

figure 170

Bell Palsy,

figure 171

Berger Disease,

figure 172

Beriberi,

figure 173

Bernard-Soulier Syndrome,

figure 174

Berylliosis,

figure 175

Biliary Atresia,

figure 176

Biotinidase Deficiency,

figure 177

Bipolar Disorder,

figure 178

Birt-Hogg-Dube Syndrome,

figure 179

Bladder Cancer,

figure 180

Bladder Exstrophy,

figure 181

Blepharitis,

figure 182

Blepharoptosis,

figure 183

Blepharospasm,

figure 184

Blindness,

figure 185

Blister,

figure 186

Bloch-Sulzberger Syndrome,

figure 187

Blood Coagulation Disorders,

figure 188

Blood Pressure, High,

figure 189

Blood Pressure, Low, Hypotension,

figure 190

Bloom Syndrome,

figure 191

Blue Rubber Bleb Nevus Syndrome,

figure 192

Boils,

figure 193

Bone Marrow Fibrosis,

figure 194

Botulism,

figure 195

Bowel obstruction,

figure 196

Bowen's Disease,

figure 197

Bradycardia,

figure 198

Brain Concussion,

figure 199

Breast Cancer,

figure 200

Breast Tumors,

figure 201

Briquet Syndrome,

figure 202

Brittle Nails,

figure 203

Bronchiolitis,

figure 204

Bronchitis,

figure 205

Bruxism, Teeth Grinding,

figure 206

Brown-Sequard Syndrome,

figure 207

Budd-Chiari syndrome,

figure 208

Buerger's Disease,

figure 209

Bulbar Palsy, Fazio-Londe Syndrome,

figure 210

Bunions, Hallux Valgus,

figure 211

Burkitt Lymphoma,

figure 212

Burning Mouth Syndrome,

figure 213

Burns,

figure 214

Bursitis,

figure 215

Cafe-au-Lait Spots,

figure 216

Caffey-De Toni-Silvermann Syndrome,

figure 217

Canavan Disease,

figure 218

Candidiasis, Vulvovaginal,

figure 219

Canker Sore,

figure 220

Carbohydrate-Deficient Glycoprotein Syndrome,

figure 221

Carcinoid Tumor,

figure 222

Carcinoma,

figure 223

Carcinoma, Merkel Cell,

figure 224

Carcinoma, Small Cell,

figure 225

Cardiac Tamponade,

figure 226

Cardiomegaly,

figure 227

Cardiomyopathy,

figure 228

Caroli Disease,

figure 229

Carotid Stenosis, Ulcer,

figure 230

Carpal Tunnel Syndrome,

figure 231

Cat Eye Syndrome,

figure 232

Cat-Scratch Disease,

figure 233

Cataract,

figure 234

Celiac Disease,

figure 235

Cellulitis,

figure 236

Central Cord Syndrome,

figure 237

Cerebellar Ataxia,

figure 238

Cerebral Hemorrhage,

figure 239

Cerebral Palsy,

figure 240

Cervix Dysplasia,

figure 241

Cervix Incompetence,

figure 242

Cesarean Section, before and after,

figure 243

Cestode Infections,

figure 244

Chalazion,

figure 245

Chancroid,

figure 246

Charcot-Marie-Tooth Disease,

figure 247

Charge Syndrome,

figure 248

Chediak-Higashi Syndrome,

figure 249

Cheilitis,

figure 250

Cherubism,

figure 251

Chest Pain,

figure 252

Chickenpox,

figure 253

Chlamydia,

figure 254

Chloasma,

figure 255

Cholangitis,

figure 256

Cholecystitis,

figure 257

Choledochal Cyst,

figure 258

Cholera,

figure 259

Cholesteatoma, Middle Ear,

figure 260

Cholesterol Embolism,

figure 261

Chondroma,

figure 262

Chondrosarcoma,

figure 263

Chordoma,

figure 264

Chorioretinitis,

figure 265

Choroideremia,

figure 266

Churg-Strauss Syndrome,

figure 267

Claudication,

figure 268

Cleft Lip,

figure 269

Clubfoot,

figure 270

Cold Sore,

figure 271

Colic,

figure 272

Coloboma,

figure 273

Color Blindness,

figure 274

Colorectal Cancer,

figure 275

Common Cold,

figure 276

Compartment Syndromes,

figure 277

Constipation,

figure 278

Convulsions,

figure 279

Costello Syndrome,

figure 280

Cough,

figure 281

Cowden's Disease,

figure 282

Cows Disease, Mad,

figure 283

Cramp,

figure 284

Craniosynostosis,

figure 285

Cretinism,

figure 286

Creutzfeldt-Jakob Syndrome,

figure 287

Cri-du-Chat Syndrome,

figure 288

Crohn's Disease,

figure 289

Croup,

figure 290

Cryoglobulinemia,

figure 291

Cryptococcosis,

figure 292

Cryptosporidiosis,

figure 293

Cubital Tunnel Syndrome,

figure 294

Currarino Syndrome,

figure 295

Cushing Syndrome,

figure 296

Cutis Laxa,

figure 297

Cyanosis,

figure 298

Cyclosporiasis,

figure 299

Cyclothymic Disorder,

figure 300

Cystic Fibrosis,

figure 301

Cysticercosis,

figure 302

Cystinosis,

figure 303

Cysts,

figure 304

Dandy-Walker Syndrome,

figure 305

Darier Disease,

figure 306

De Lange Syndrome,

figure 307

de Quervain's Tendinitis ,

figure 308

Deafness,

figure 309

Dehydration,

figure 310

Dejerine-Roussy Syndrome,

figure 311

Dejerine-Sottas Disease,

figure 312

Dejerine-Thomas Syndrome,

figure 313

Dementia, Vascular,

figure 314

Dengue Fever,

figure 315

Dentigerous Cyst,

figure 316

Dermatofibroma,

figure 317

Dermatomyositis,

figure 318

Dermatosis,

figure 319

Dermoid Cyst,

figure 320

Desmoid Tumor,

figure 321

Devic's disease, Syndrome,

figure 322

Diabetes Insipidus,

figure 323

Diabetes Type 1,

figure 324

Diabetes Type 2,

figure 325

Diaper Rash,

figure 326

DiGeorge Syndrome,

figure 327

Digestive Problems,

figure 328

Digestive System Cancer,

figure 329

Diphtheria,

figure 330

Distal Trisomy 10q,

figure 331

Distichiasis,

figure 332

Diverticulitis,

figure 333

Dizziness,

figure 334

Double Vision, Diplopia,

figure 335

Down Syndrome,

figure 336

Drooling, Sialorrhea,

figure 337

Dry Eye Syndrome,

figure 338

Dry Mouth, Xerostomia,

figure 339

Duane Syndrome,

figure 340

Duodenal Ulcer,

figure 341

Dupuytren Contracture,

figure 342

Dysentery,

figure 343

Dyslexia,

figure 344

Dystocia,

figure 345

Dystonia,

figure 346

Ear Neoplasms, Cancer,

figure 347

Eating Disorders,

figure 348

Ebstein's Anomaly,

figure 349

Eclampsia,

figure 350

Ectodermal Dysplasia,

figure 351

Ectropion,

figure 352

Eczema,

figure 353

Edema,

figure 354

Ehlers-Danlos Syndrome,

figure 355

Eisenmenger's Syndrome,

figure 356

Elephant Man Disease, Proteus Syndrome,

figure 357

Ellis-van Creveld Syndrome,

figure 358

Embolism, Cholesterol,

figure 359

Emphysema,

figure 360

Empty Sella Syndrome,

figure 361

Empyema, Pleural,

figure 362

Encephalitis,

figure 363

Encephalocele,

figure 364

Encopresis,

figure 365

Endocrine Gland Cancer,

figure 366

Endometriosis,

figure 367

Entropion,

figure 368

Eosinophilia,

figure 369

Epidermal Cyst,

figure 370

Epididymitis,

figure 371

Epiglottitis,

figure 372

Epilepsy,

figure 373

Erb's Palsy,

figure 374

Erdheim-Chester Disease,

figure 375

Erysipelas,

figure 376

Erythema,

figure 377

Esophageal Achalasia,

figure 378

Esophageal Atresia,

figure 379

Esophageal Cancer,

figure 380

Essential Tremor,

figure 381

Evans Syndrome,

figure 382

Ewing's Sarcoma,

figure 383

Exfoliation Syndrome,

figure 384

Exfoliative Dermatitis,

figure 385

Exotropia,

figure 386

Eye Cancer,

figure 387

Eye Hemorrhage,

figure 388

Fabry Disease,

figure 389

Facial Asymmetry,

figure 390

Facial Paralysis,

figure 391

Fanconi Anemia,

figure 392

Farsightedness, Hyperopia,

figure 393

Fatigue,

figure 394

Fatigue Syndrome,

figure 395

Fatty Liver,

figure 396

Favism,

figure 397

Fecal Incontinence,

figure 398

Fever,

figure 399

Fibrocystic Breast Disease,

figure 400

Fibroid Tumor,

figure 401

Fibromuscular Dysplasia,

figure 402

Fibromyalgia Syndrome,

figure 403

Fibrosis,

figure 404

Fifth Disease,

figure 405

Fish Odor Syndrome,

figure 406

Flatulence,

figure 407

Fournier Gangrene,

figure 408

Freeman-Sheldon Syndrome,

figure 409

Freiberg's disease,

figure 410

Friedreich Ataxia,

figure 411

Frostbite,

figure 412

Fucosidosis,

figure 413

Funnel Chest,

figure 414

G6PD Deficiency, figure 415

Gait Disorders, figure 416

Galactosemias, figure 417

Gallbladder Cancer,

figure 418

Gallbladder Inflammation,

figure 419

Gallstones,

figure 420

Gangrene,

figure 421

Gas Gangrene,

figure 422

Gastric Cancer,

figure 423

Gastritis,

figure 424

Gastrointestinal Hemorrhage,

figure 425

Gastroparesis,

figure 426

Gaucher Disease,

figure 427

German Measles, Rubella,

figure 428

Giant Lymph Node Hyperplasia,

figure 429

Giardiasis,

figure 430

Gingivitis,

figure 431

Glanzmann Thrombasthenia,

figure 432

Glaucoma,

figure 433

Glioblastoma,

figure 434

Glioma,

figure 435

Glomerulonephritis,

figure 436

Glossitis,

figure 437

Glycogen Storage Disease,

figure 438

Goldenhar Syndrome,

figure 439

Gonorrhea,

figure 440

Goodpasture Syndrome,

figure 441

Gorlin Goltz Syndrome,

figure 442

Gout,

figure 443

Granuloma,

figure 444

Graves' Disease,

figure 445

Guillain-Barre Syndrome,

figure 446

Gynecomastia,

figure 447

Gyrate Atrophy,

figure 448

Hailey-Hailey Disease,

figure 449

Hakim Syndrome,

figure 450

Halitosis, Bad Breath,

figure 451

Hallervorden-Spatz Syndrome,

figure 452

Hallucinations,

figure 453

Hammertoes,

figure 454

Hand-Schuller-Christian disease,

figure 455

Hartnup Disease,

figure 456

Head and Neck Cancer,

figure 457

Headache,

figure 458

Hearing Loss,

figure 459

Heart Block,

figure 460

Heartburn,

figure 461

Heat Stroke,

figure 462

HELLP Syndrome,

figure 463

Hemangioma,

figure 464

Hematuria,

figure 465

Hemianopsia,

figure 466

Hemifacial Microsomia,

figure 467

Hemiplegia,

figure 468

Hemochromatosis,

figure 469

Hemolytic-Uremic Syndrome,

figure 470

Hemophilia,

figure 471

Hemoptysis,

figure 472

Hemorrhage,

figure 473

Hemorrhoids,

figure 474

Hepatitis,

figure 475

Hermansky Pudlak Syndrome,

figure 476

Hermaphroditism,

figure 477

Hernia,

figure 478

Hernia, Diaphragmatic,

figure 479

Hernia, Hiatal,

figure 480

Herniated Disk,

figure 481

Herpes,

figure 482

Hip Dislocation,

figure 483

Hirschsprung Disease,

figure 484

Hirsutism,

figure 485

Histidinemia,

figure 486

HIV Infections,

figure 487

Hodgkin Disease,

figure 488

Holoprosencephaly,

figure 489

Homocystinuria,

figure 490

Horner Syndrome,

figure 491

Huntington Disease,

figure 492

Hutchinson-Gilford Syndrome, Progeria,

figure 493

Hutchinson's Melanotic Freckle,

figure 494

Hydrocephalus,

figure 495

Hydronephrosis,

figure 496

Hyperacusis,

figure 497

Hyperaldosteronism,

figure 498

Hypercalcemia,

figure 499

Hyperemesis Gravidarum, Pregnancy,

figure 500

Hyperemia, Reactive,

figure 501

Hyperhidrosis,

figure 502

Hyperinsulinism,

figure 503

Hyperlipidemia,

figure 504

Hyperostosis,

figure 505

Hyperoxaluria,

figure 506

Hyperprolactinemia,

figure 507

Hyperthyroidism,

figure 508

Hyperventilation,

figure 509

Hypervitaminosis A,

figure 510

Hyphema,

figure 511

Hypocalcemia,

figure 512

Hypochondriasis,

figure 513

Hypoglycemia,

figure 514

Hypogonadism,

figure 515

Hypohidrosis,

figure 516

Hypokalemia,

figure 517

Hyponatremia,

figure 518

Hypopituitarism,

figure 519

Hypospadias,

figure 520

Hypothermia,

figure 521

Hypothyroidism,

figure 522

Ichthyosis,

figure 523

IgA Deficiency,

figure 524

Immersion Foot,

figure 525

Impetigo,

figure 526

Impotence,

figure 527

Indigestion, Dyspepsia,

figure 528

Infertility, Female,

figure 529

Infertility, Male,

figure 530

Inflammation,

figure 531

Influenza,

figure 532

Insulin Resistance,

figure 533

Insulinoma,

figure 534

Interstitial Cystitis, Painful Bladder Syndrome,

figure 535

Intestinal Polyps, Gardner Syndrome,

figure 536

Intestines Cancer,

figure 537

Intracranial Aneurysm,

figure 538

Iritis,

figure 539

Iron Overload,

figure 540

Isaacs' Syndrome,

figure 541

Jacobsen Syndrome,

figure 542

Jaundice,

figure 543

Job's Syndrome,

figure 544

Jock Itch,

figure 545

Juvenile Psoriatic Arthritis,

figure 546

Kabuki Syndrome,

figure 547

Kallmann's Syndrome,

figure 548

Kartagener Syndrome,

figure 549

Kawasaki Disease, Mucocutaneous Lymph Node Syndrome,

figure 550

Kearns-Sayer Syndrome,

figure 551

Keratitis,

figure 552

Keratoconus,

figure 553

Kernicterus,

figure 554

Kidney Failure,

figure 555

Kidney, Medullary Sponge,

figure 556

Kidney Stones, Calculi,

figure 557

Kidney Tubular Necrosis,

figure 558

Kleine-Levin Syndrome,

figure 559

Kleptomania,

figure 560

Klinefelter Syndrome,

figure 561

Klippel-Feil Syndrome, KFS,

figure 562

Klippel-Trenaunay-Weber Syndrome,

figure 563

Klumpke's Palsy,

figure 564

Koilonychia, Nail,

figure 565

Kuru,

figure 566

Labyrinthitis,

figure 567

Lactation Disorders,

figure 568

Lactose Intolerance,

figure 569

Lambert-Eaton Myasthenic Syndrome,

figure 570

Landau-Kleffner Syndrome,

figure 571

Langer-Giedion Syndrome,

figure 572

Larsen Syndrome,

figure 573

Laryngitis,

figure 574

Laryngostenosis,

figure 575

Larynx Cancer,

figure 576

Lassa Fever,

figure 577

Lateral Medullary Syndrome,

figure 578

Latex-Fruit Syndrome,

figure 579

Laurence-Moon Syndrome,

figure 580

Lead Poisoning,

figure 581

Leg Ulcer,

figure 582

Legg-Calve-Perthes Disease, LCPD,

figure 583

Legg-Perthes Disease,

figure 584

Legionnaires' Disease,

figure 585

Leigh Syndrome,

figure 586

Leiomyoma,

figure 587

Leiomyosarcoma, Intestinal,

figure 588

Lentigo,

figure 589

Leprosy, Hansen's Disease,

figure 590

Leptospirosis,

figure 591

Lesch-Nyhan Syndrome,

figure 592

Leuconychia, Nail,

figure 593

Leukemia,

figure 594

Leukopenia,

figure 595

Lewy Body Disease,

figure 596

Lichen Planus,

figure 597

Lichen Sclerosus, White Spot Disease,

figure 598

Lipodystrophy,

figure 599

Lipoma,

figure 600

Lissencephaly,

figure 601

Liver Cancer, Hematoma,

figure 602

Liver Cirrhosis,

figure 603

Long QT Syndrome,

figure 604

Lordosis,

figure 605

Louis-Bar Syndrome,

figure 606

Lowe Syndrome,

figure 607

Ludwig's Angina,

figure 608

Lupus,

figure 609

Lymphadenitis,

figure 610

Lymphangioma,

figure 611

Lymphangiomyomatosis,

figure 612

Lymphogranuloma Venereum,

figure 613

Lymphoma,

figure 614

Lymphoma, Non-Hodgkin,

figure 615

Machado-Joseph Disease,

figure 616

Macroglossia,

figure 617

Macular Degeneration,

figure 618

Madura Foot,

figure 619

Malaria,

figure 620

Maple Syrup Urine Disease,

figure 621

Marfan Syndrome,

figure 622

Martin-Bell Syndrome, Fragile X Syndrome,

figure 623

Mastocytosis,

figure 624

Mastoiditis,

figure 625

McCune-Albright syndrome,

figure 626

Measles,

figure 627

Meckel's Diverticulum,

figure 628

Meconium Aspiration,

figure 629

Mediastinal Cyst,

figure 630

Mediterranean Fever, Familial, FMF,

figure 631

Medulloblastoma,

figure 632

Meige Syndrome,

figure 633

Melanonychia, Nail,

figure 634

MELAS Syndrome,

figure 635

Melkersson-Rosenthal Syndrome,

figure 636

Melorheostosis,

figure 637

Meniere's Disease,

figure 638

Meningioma,

figure 639

Meningitis,

figure 640

Menkes Kinky Hair Syndrome,

figure 641

Metabolic Syndrome X,

figure 642

Methemoglobinemia,

figure 643

Microcephaly,

figure 644

Migraine Headache,

figure 645

Miller Fisher Syndrome,

figure 646

Miscarriage,

figure 647

Mite Infestations,

figure 648

Mitral Valve Prolapse,

figure 649

Mixed Connective Tissue Disease,

figure 650

Motion Sickness,

figure 651

Mouth Cancer,

figure 652

Moyamoya Disease,

figure 653

Mucopolysaccharidoses,

figure 654

Multiple Hereditary Exostoses, MHE,

figure 655

Multiple Myeloma,

figure 656

Multiple Personality Disorder,

figure 657

Multiple Sclerosis,

figure 658

Multiple System Atrophy,

figure 659

Mumps,

figure 660

Munchausen Syndrome,

figure 661

Muscle Cramp,

figure 662

Muscle Spasticity,

figure 663

Muscular Atrophy,

figure 664

Myasthenia Gravis,

figure 665

Myelitis,

figure 666

Myelodysplastic Syndromes,

figure 667

Myelofibrosis,

figure 668

Myeloid Metaplasia,

figure 669

Myocarditis,

figure 670

Myoclonus,

figure 671

Myoma,

figure 672

Myopathies,

figure 673

Myopia,

figure 674

Myositis,

figure 675

Myositis Ossificans,

figure 676

Myxoma,

figure 677

Nail-Patella Syndrome,

figure 678

Nails, Ingrown,

figure 679

Narcolepsy,

figure 680

Nasal Obstruction,

figure 681

Nasal Polyps,

figure 682

Neck Pain,

figure 683

Necrotizing Fascitis,

figure 684

Nelson Syndrome,

figure 685

Nerve Compression Syndromes,

figure 686

Neuralgia,

figure 687

Neurofibromatoses,

figure 688

Neuromuscular Diseases,

figure 689

Niemann-Pick Diseases,

figure 690

Noonan Syndrome,

figure 691

Nosebleed,

figure 692

Nystagmus,

figure 693

Ocular Albinism,

figure 694

Oculocerebrorenal Syndrome,

figure 695

Oliguria,

figure 696

Olivopontocerebellar Atrophies,

figure 697

Ollier Disease,

figure 698

Onchocerciasis,

figure 699

Onychatrophia, Nail,

figure 700

Onychauxis, Nail,

figure 701

Onychomycosis,

figure 702

Onychorrhexis, Nail,

figure 703

Ophthalmoplegia,

figure 704

Optic Atrophies,

figure 705

Optic Neuritis,

figure 706

Optic Neuropathy, Ischemic,

figure 707

Osteoarthritis,

figure 708

Osteochondritis,

figure 709

Osteogenesis Imperfecta,

figure 710

Osteomalacia,

figure 711

Osteomyelitis,

figure 712

Osteonecrosis,

figure 713

Osteopetrosis,

figure 714

Osteoporosis,

figure 715

Osteosarcoma,

figure 716

Otosclerosis,

figure 717

Ovarian Cysts,

figure 718

Ovary Cancer,

figure 719

Owren's Disease, Parahemophilia,

figure 720

Paget's Disease,

figure 721

Paget's Disease,

Mammary, figure 722

Painful Sexual Intercourse, Dyspareunia,

figure 723

Pallister-Killian Syndrome,

figure 724

Pancreas Cancer,

figure 725

Pancreatitis,

figure 726

Papilledema,

figure 727

Papilloma,

figure 728

Paraganglioma,

figure 729

Paraneoplastic Syndromes, Nervous System,

figure 730

Parkinson Disease,

figure 731

Paronychia, Nail,

figure 732

Parsonage-Turner Syndrome,

figure 733

Pellagra,

figure 734

Pelvic Inflammatory Disease,

figure 735

Pemphigoid, Bullous,

figure 736

Pemphigus,

figure 737

Penile Induration,

figure 738

Peptic Ulcer,

figure 739

Peroxisomal Disorders,

figure 740

Peutz-Jeghers Syndrome,

figure 741

Peyronie's Disease,

figure 742

Phenylketonurias, PKU,

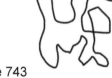

figure 743

Phlebitis,

figure 744

Photosensitivity Disorders,

figure 745

Pierre Robin Syndrome,

figure 746

Pilonidal Cysts,

figure 747

Pituitary Diseases,

figure 748

Plantar Fasciitis,

figure 749

Pleurisy,

figure 750

Pneumonia,

figure 751

Pneumothorax,

figure 752

POEMS Syndrome,

figure 753

Poland's Syndrome,

figure 754

Polio,

figure 755

Polyarteritis Nodosa,

figure 756

Polychondritis, Relapsing,

figure 757

Polycystic Ovary Syndrome,

figure 758

Polycythemia Vera,

figure 759

Polyhydramnios,

figure 760

Polymyalgia Rheumatica,

figure 761

Polymyositis,

figure 762

Polyneuropathies,

figure 763

Postpartum Hemorrhage,

figure 764

Postpoliomyelitis Syndrome,

figure 765

Prader-Willi Syndrome,

figure 766

Pregnancy and Gestational Diabetes,

figure 767

Pregnancy, Ectopic,

figure 768

Presbycusis,

figure 769

Presbyopia,

figure 770

Pressure Sores,

figure 771

Priapism,

figure 772

Primary Lateral Sclerosis, PLS,

figure 773

Proctitis,

figure 774

Prostate Cancer,

figure 775

Proteinuria,

figure 776

Proteus Syndrome,

figure 777

Prune Belly Syndrome,

figure 778

Pruritus,

figure 779

Pruritus Vulvae,

figure 780

Pseudomembranous Colitis,

figure 781

Pseudomonas, Nail,

figure 782

Pseudomyxoma Peritonei,

figure 783

Pseudoxanthoma   Elasticum,   Gronblad-Strandberg
Syndrome,

figure 784

Psoriasis,

figure 785

Psoriasis, Nail,

figure 786

Pterygium,

figure 787

Pterygium, Nail,

figure 788

Pterygium Inversum Unguis, Nail,

figure 789

Pulmonary Atresia,

figure 790

Pulmonary Fibrosis,

figure 791

Pupil Disorders,

figure 792

Purpura, Schoenlein-Henoch,

figure 793

Pyelonephritis,

figure 794

Pyoderma Gangrenosum,

figure 795

Q Fever,

figure 796

Quadriplegia,

figure 797

Rabies,

figure 798

Raynaud Disease,

figure 799

Rectal Prolapse,

figure 800

Reflex Sympathetic Dystrophy,

figure 801

Refsum Disease,

figure 802

Reiter's Syndrome,

figure 803

Respiratory Distress Syndrome, Newborn,

figure 804

Restless Legs Syndrome, Ekborn Syndrome,

figure 805

Retinal Detachment,

figure 806

Retinitis Pigmentosa,

figure 807

Retinoblastoma,

figure 808

Retinoschisis,

figure 809

Retroperitoneal Fibrosis,

figure 810

Rett Syndrome,

figure 811

Reye Syndrome,

figure 812

Rhabdoid Tumor,

figure 813

Rhabdomyolysis,

figure 814

Rhabdomyosarcoma,

figure 815

Rheumatic Fever,

figure 816

Rheumatoid Arthritis,

figure 817

Rhinitis,

figure 818

Rhinoscleroma,

figure 819

Rickets,

figure 820

Robinow Syndrome,

figure 821

Romberg Syndrome,

figure 822

Rosacea,

figure 823

Rosenthal Syndrome,

figure 824

Rubinstein-Taybi Syndrome,

figure 825

Russell Silver Syndrome,

figure 826

Salpingitis,

figure 827

Samter's Syndrome,

figure 828

Sandfly Fever, Pappataci Fever,

figure 829

Sandhoff Disease,

figure 830

SAPHO syndrome,

figure 831

Sarcoidosis,

figure 832

Schistosomiasis, bilharzias,

figure 833

Schizophrenia,

figure 834

Sciatica,

figure 835

Scimitar Syndrome,

figure 836

Scleritis,

figure 837

Scoliosis,

figure 838

Scotoma,

figure 839

Scurvy,

figure 840

Seborrheic Keratosis,

figure 841

Sepsis Syndrome,

figure 842

Septo-Optic Dysplasia,

figure 843

Sex Chromosome Aberrations,

figure 844

Sezary Syndrome,

figure 845

Shaken Baby Syndrome,

figure 846

Shingles, Herpes Zoster,

figure 847

Short Bowel Syndrome,

figure 848

Shwachman-Diamond syndrome,

figure 849

Shy-Drager Syndrome,

figure 850

Sick Building Syndrome,

figure 851

Sinusitis,

figure 852

Sjogren's Syndrome,

figure 853

Skeletal Dysplasias,

figure 854

Skin Cancer,

figure 855

Skin Ulcer,

figure 856

Small Intestine Cancer,

figure 857

Smallpox,

figure 858

Smith-Lemli-Opitz Syndrome, RSH,

figure 859

Sneddon Syndrome,

figure 860

Snoring,

figure 861

Sore Throat, Pharyngitis,

figure 862

Speech Disorders,

figure 863

Spermatic Cord Torsion,

figure 864

Spina Bifida,

figure 865

Spinal Muscular Atrophies, SMA,

figure 866

Spinal Stenosis,

figure 867

Splenic Rupture,

figure 868

Spondylitis,

figure 869

Spots and Floaters,

figure 870

Sprengel's Deformity,

figure 871

Stevens-Johnson Syndrome,

figure 872

Stickler Syndrome,

figure 873

Stiff Man Syndrome,

figure 874

Stomatitis, Aphthous, canker sore,

figure 875

Strabismus,

figure 876

Strongyloidiasis,

figure 877

Sturge-Weber Syndrome,

figure 878

Styes,

figure 879

Subacute Sclerosing Panencephalitis,

figure 880

Superior Vena Cava Syndrome,

figure 881

Swallowing Disorders,

figure 882

Sweet's Syndrome,

figure 883

Synovitis,

figure 884

Syphilis,

figure 885

Tachycardia,

figure 886

Takayasu's Arteritis,

figure 887

Tangier Disease,

figure 888

Tay-Sachs Disease,

figure 889

Tear Ducts, Blocked,

figure 890

Temporal Arteritis,

figure 891

Tendinitis,

figure 892

Tennis Elbow,

figure 893

Tenosynovitis,

figure 894

Teratoma,

figure 895

Tetanus,

figure 896

Tetralogy of Fallot,

figure 897

Thanatophoric Dysplasia,

figure 898

Thoracic Outlet Syndrome,

figure 899

Three-day-fever, Roseola Infantum,

figure 900

Thrombocytopenia,

figure 901

Thymoma,

figure 902

Thyroid Cancer,

figure 903

Thyroid Hormone Resistance Syndrome,

figure 904

Thyroiditis,

figure 905

Tietze's Syndrome,

figure 906

Tinea Unguis, Nail,

figure 907

Tinnitus,

figure 908

TMJ Syndrome,

figure 909

Tonsillitis,

figure 910

Torticollis,

figure 911

Tourette Syndrome,

figure 912

Tracheo Laryngomalacia,

figure 913

Trachoma,

figure 914

Treacher Collins Syndorme,

figure 915

Tremor,

figure 916

Tricuspid Atresia,

figure 917

Trismus,

figure 918

Tuberculosis,

figure 919

Turner Syndrome,

figure 920

Tympanic Membrane Perforation,

figure 921

Typhoid Fever,

figure 922

Typhus,

figure 923

Tyrosinemia,

figure 924

Ulcerative Colitis,

figure 925

Undescended testicles,

figure 926

Urethral Stenosis,

figure 927

Urethritis,

figure 928

Urinary Retention,

figure 929

Urinary Tract Cancer,

figure 930

Urticaria,

figure 931

Uterus Cancer,

figure 932

Uveitis,

figure 933

Van Lohuizen Syndrome,

figure 934

Varicose Veins,

figure 935

Vasculitis,

figure 936

Vertical Ridges, Nail,

figure 937

Vesico-Ureteral Reflux,

figure 938

Vestibular Neuronitis,

figure 939

Vitiligo,

figure 940

Vocal Cord Paralysis,

figure 941

Vogt-Koyanagi-Harada syndrome,

figure 942

Voice Disorders,

figure 943

Vomiting,

figure 944

Von Hippel-Lindau syndrome,

figure 945

von Willebrand Disease,

figure 946

Waardenburg's Syndrome,

figure 947

Waldenstrom Macroglobulinemia,

figure 948

Wallenberg Syndrome,

figure 949

Warts,

figure 950

Weber-Christian disease,

figure 951

Wegener's Granulomatosis,

figure 952

Werner Syndrome,

figure 953

Wernicke-Korsakoff Syndrome,

figure 954

West Nile Fever,

figure 955

West Syndrome,

figure 956

Whipple Disease,

figure 957

Whooping Cough,

figure 958

Williams Syndrome,

figure 969

Wilms' Tumor,

figure 960

Wilson's Disease, Hepatolenticular Degeneration,

figure 961

Wiskott-Aldrich Syndrome,

figure 962

Wolff-Parkinson-White Syndrome,

figure 963

Wolfram Syndrome,

figure 964

Wolman Disease,

figure 965

Xanthoma,

figure 966

Xeroderma Pigmentosum,

figure 967

Xerostomia, Hyposalivation,

figure 968

XYY Karyotype,

figure 969

Yaws,

figure 970

Yellow Fever,

figure 971

Zellweger Syndrome,

figure 972

Zenker Diverticulum,

figure 973

Human body parts and Organs

Hair,

figure 974

Forehead,

figure 975

Top of the head,

figure 976

Head, back,

figure 977

Head, left side,

figure 978

Head, right side,

figure 979

Eyebrows, left,

figure 980

Eyebrows, right,

figure 981

Eye, left,

figure 982

Eye, right,

figure 983

Eyelashes, left,

figure 984

Eyelashes, right,

figure 985

Nose,

figure 986

Cheek, left,

figure 987

Cheek, right,

figure 988

Ear, left,

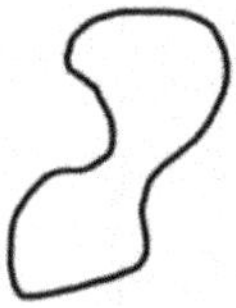

figure 989

Ear, right,

figure 990

Mouth and lips,

figure 991

Tongue,

figure 992

Gums, lower,

figure 993

Gums, upper,

figure 994

Teeth, lower,

figure 995

Teeth, upper,

figure 996

Throat,

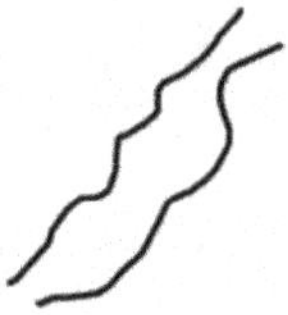

figure 997

Neck,

figure 998

Shoulder, left,

figure 999

Shoulder, right,

figure 1000

Armpit, left,

figure 1001

Armpit, right,

figure 1002

Arms, left,

figure 1003

Arms, right,

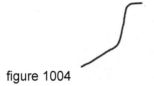

figure 1004

Hand, left,

figure 1005

Hand, right,

figure 1006

Fingers, left,

figure 1007

Fingers, right,

figure 1008

Chest,

figure 1009

Breast, left,

figure 1010

Breast, right,

figure 1011

Stomach,

figure 1012

Small intestine,

figure1013

Large intestine,

figure 1014

Rectum,

figure 1015

Scrotum,

figure 1016

Gall bladder,

figure 1017

Pancreas,

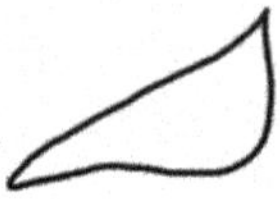

figure 1018

Liver,

figure 1019

Kidney, left,

figure 1020

Kidney, right,

figure 1021

Heart,

figure 1022

Thigh, left,

figure 1023

Thigh, right,

figure 1024

Knee, left,

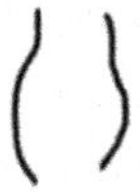

figure 1025

Knee, right,

figure 1026

Shin, left,

figure 1027

Shin, right,

figure 1028

Foot, left,

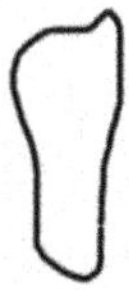

figure 1029

Foot, right,

figure 1030

Heel, left,

figure 1031

Heel, right,

figure 1032

Toes, left,

figure 1033

Toes, right,

figure 1034

Upper back,

figure 1035

Mid back,

figure 1036

Lower back,

figure 1037

Genital organs, male,

figure 1038

Genital organs, female,

figure 1039

Chapter 41

Preventative Measures and Daily Power Exercises

The best way to explain preventative measures is by examples of daily tasks to do, for the ultimate result of having a good normal functioning S.H.E.

Use the TEENS concept for starting the day, by bringing one or more of the five images to mind as soon as you wake up.

Do energy balance check on you and detect the breaks in the electromagnetic field, and fix them as you wake up and as you go to sleep, don't wait for symptoms to occur.

Be a pollution counter and watch your thoughts and what you say at all times, if you live with others or family, explain the concept and rotate turns of who will be the pollution counter, this will help reduce that type of pollution and could reach the stage of elimination of that pollution.

Always project good energy to all people, all animals, and all plants whenever you can, as we said earlier you project good, you get good, build up your reserves for your S.H.E.

Listen to others when they talk to you and help them and correct any thought pollution projected in the conversation.

Mentally create a video film of what you want and play it as many times as needed, and change it when you need to and always have that video available to you. It only takes seconds to play the video in your mind, so it is quite easy.

Eliminate pollution whenever and wherever you encounter it, I realize some pollution you can eliminate and others you will not be able to eliminate and in this latter case use a protective shield.

Devise your own way of daily tasks to do for your own benefit.

All the above is within your capabilities and could be done in 10 minutes every day, remember that you have 1440 minutes every day, so really 10 minutes is less than 1% of your day, and the return on investment is a million fold or more by being in good health and having your S.H.E. functioning normally for your well being.

Chapter 42

Stress

We mentioned earlier that everyone has an upper limit and a lower limit, for all types of emotions, activities, and whatever you are involved with. You can have different upper and lower limits for different situations.

Anything falling within those limits never creates stress, anything falling beyond those limits either above or below, will cause stress, stress in itself is self induced, as some things could be stressful to some and not stressful to others.

When we are faced by something outside our limits, it is our choice how we deal with it, we can be stressed and negatively affect ourselves and our S.H.E or just treat it as another different occurrence of something that doesn't happen very often, we just deal with it favorably.

Unfortunately the word stress is used by whoever presents you with a solution, they say you are stressed, so you need their services or goods, so for many the more the stress the merrier it is, but it shouldn't be like that for you, it is definitely not like that for me.

I just look at what others call stress as a different situation that might take longer than other activities to pass by, and there is a way to make things better, just a matter of finding that way, that firm belief that there is a way, makes you find it, you have placed that desire within the ultra-conscious and the master chip, so they will work to find that way for you, it is as simple as that.

Remember that the stressed person harms themselves first then their loved ones next, so by simple logic you don't want to harm yourself, and most definitely you don't want to harm your loved ones.

The word desserts is stressed spelled backward, always remember the word desserts and how happy you are when you get desserts, keep that word association in mind.

Stress is another type of thought and or action pollution, that affects your S.H.E., and so many studies have been done that show the devastating effect of desserts – this is intentional to write desserts instead of stressed – of course all what they show in the studies could happen, because your S.H.E. has been affected and it doesn't function as it should be.

It is your life and your S.H.E., and as much as you are careful with visible pollution, be as diligent with whatever affects negatively your S.H.E., specially the invisible pollution.

Another simple way to get rid of desserts, write the issue that is upsetting you on a small piece of paper and flush it down the toilet, by doing that you have just broken the association between you and the upsetting issue.

Last thoughts on desserts

Use the TEENS concept to relax at will

Visualize you are happy

Have your shield always up and charged

Chapter 43

Summation

All what have been discussed in the earlier chapters, collectively will help you to do energy balance, and remote viewing and a lot more, the only limiting factor is you and what you impose on yourself, so be careful not to impose restrictions on yourself, keep the door open and you will receive what is best for you.

By the way, imposing restrictions is also a type of pollution; so be careful.

First you have no idea what you are capable of, consciously you are capable of doing many things, however at the level of energy balance, you are capable of doing more, and the first step, you have already done, by reaching this part of the book, the second step is to eliminate pollution, specifically, thought pollution, third step relax, fourth step master the pendulum part, fifth step you will discover all what you are capable of, sixth step help others when you can.

I intentionally omitted or didn't mention some information, for the sole purpose that it is a lot more beneficial for you as the reader to arrive at those conclusions, your conclusions are more important to you than my conclusions, however I provided comprehensive guidelines to enable you to learn energy balance and other methods, and where you go from here is entirely up to you, I sincerely hope that you enjoyed the book and found the explanations simple, and managed to do energy balance and the other methods as well.

Chapter 44

Recommended Reading

This book is quite sufficient for you to start doing energy balance, however the books I am recommending here, are the books I have read, and I am sure they all helped me perform all the various energy balance methods I outlined, and quite a few of them were originally recommended to me by my teacher and friend Vince Kaye.

A good source for books is Amazon, where you can also have the opportunity to buy used books in very good condition.

Another good source is the Friends of the Library Sales, in many places in the Public Libraries in the USA they have this group, and I have found there very good books at very reasonable prices, check with your public library.

Energy Medicine by Donna Eden, outlines the meridians of various body parts and how to use them, also a very good chapter on Magnets and effects of electropollution.

Human Body, very good illustrations of body parts and how they work, very useful for use with pendulum.

Psychic Powers by Denning and Phillips

How to Heal with Color, by Ted Andrews, explains the subject in simple terms.

Aura Reading for beginners, by Richard Webster, it helped me see the aura and its colors.

Dowsing for Beginners, by Richard Webster, helped me understand more regarding dowsing.

Scrying for Beginners, by Donald Tyson.

Color Therapy, by Reuben Amber.

The Psychic Healing Book, by Amy Wallace & Bill Henkin.

Denial is not a River in Egypt, by Shelley Stockwell, a lot of insight into hypnosis.

Hypnosis for beginners, by William Hewitt, this book convinced me to pursue hypnosis which enabled me to develop the TEENS concept.

How to Develop and use Psychic Touch, by Ted Andrews.

Acupressure for Common Ailments, by Chris Jarmey and John Tindall, I used the methods outlined using my mind, it helped me in identifying where to mentally use acupressure.

The Magic Power of Emotional Appeal, by Roy Garn, a must read for Teenagers and adults, you will learn a lot.

Develop your Psychic Skills, by Enid Hoffman, increases the awareness for healing.

Graphotypes, by Sheila Kurtz & Marilyn Lester, it contains very good exercises for improving self esteem and confidence using handwriting.

Boost your Brain Power, by Ellen Michaud, Russell Wild, will definitely help to understand brain power.

Acupuncture without Needles, by J.V. Cerney, very informative about the subject.

Creative Visualization, by Denning & Phillips, helps you understand more about the power of visualization.

Crystal Balls & Crystal Bowls, by Ted Andrews, it shows you the abilities of the mind once you open the door for more information.

Helping Yourself with Numerology, by Helyn Hitchcock, a very good book on numerology.

Hidden Power, How to Unleash The Power of Your Subconscious Mind, by James K. Van Fleet, very good book on the subject.

The Therapeutic Touch, How to use your hands to help or to heal, by Dolores Krieger, very good insight.

Go Up And Seek God, by Vianna

Go Up and Work With God, By Vianna Stibal, Vianna's books are incredibly helpful, specially about gene replacement, I used the techniques very successfully, she knows what she is talking about.

Change Your DNA Change Your Life, Robert V. Gerard, more insight into DNA Therapy, very useful.

Ask and It Is Given, by Esther and Jerry Hicks, helps you ask for what is right for you, very good book.

The Healer's Manual, by Ted Andrews, helps you understand so many ways for healing.

The Silva Mind Control Method, by Jose Silva, very good methods for your mind control, recommended for teenagers as well as adults.

The Gift of Healing, by Gerald Loe, very easy style and informative reading from a person who has the gift.

Listening, by Lee Coit, you will know what listening can do for you.

The magic Power of Your Mind, by Walter M. Germain.

Soul Healing, by Dr. Bruce Goldberg.

Power of Thought, by Eugene Maurey, very good book on the power of thoughts, it will help you avoid thought pollution.

Numerology Magic, by Richard Webster, will help you understand people more by using the Number Square.

Music Therapy for Non-Musicians, by Ted Andrews, nobody else explains it better.

The Secret of Instantaneous Healing, by Harry Douglas Smith, a very helpful book.

The Power of Your Subconscious Mind, by Dr. Joseph Murphy, about healing.

Hypnosis How to put a Smile on Your Face and Money In Your Pocket, by Shelley Stockwell, she is a wonderful lady, very helpful and explains a great deal about hypnosis.

Atlas of The Human Body, by Takeo Takahashi, I used it a lot.

The World's best Anatomocal Charts, by Anatomical Chart Company, very clear and large diagrams of the anatomy of the human body.

Chapter 45

Web sites

The FDA web site http://www.fda.gov to know about which medications contains mercury.

http://www.mercola.com very informative web site regarding medications and health information.

http://www.lessemf.com a good source for the Trifield Meter and other equipment.

http://www.causeof.org/electro_bvoltage.htm good information regarding body voltage

http://www.curezone.com it is a forum for treatment methods for many ailments.

https://www.ozarkresearch.org The power of thought, and has a good reading list of books.

http://www.lactose.co.uk a good source for Food Additives information

http://www.foodag.com food additives guide

http://www.bau-biologieusa.com good source for pollution information

http://www.emofree.com Emotional Freedom Techniques

http://www.oroselket.com My web site

http://www.intuitivedowsing.com For purchasing pendulums

Chapter 46

Services

If you need to contact me for my services, please use email oroselket@oroselket.com with a subject line Request for help, you can include your telephone number if you wish to be contacted by telephone.

Fees for services:
- Send a check only if you feel you have received the benefit.
- Send me an amount that is in keeping with your financial situation, obligations and what you feel the service is worth.